THE
KEEPERS
OF THE
LIGHT
CODES

**A CHANNELED GUIDE TO
ENDING YOUR SPIRITUAL QUEST
AND INITIATING YOUR MASTERY**

RHIANNON HEINS

The Keepers Of The Light Codes
Heins, Rhiannon
ISBN ebook 978-0-646-86162-3
ISBN paperback 978-0-646-86150-0

CONTENTS

Preface 7

The Keepers of the Light Codes 13

THE LESSONS

LESSON 1: The Fabric of Who You Are 21

LESSON 2: Let There Be Light in Your Heart 23

LESSON 3: Open Your Heart to Love 25

LESSON 4: The Gateway to God 27

LESSON 5: The Liberation of Self 31

LESSON 6: The Start of the Next Chapter 33

LESSON 7: The Satisfaction of Knowing 37

LESSON 8: The Art of Letting Go 39

LESSON 9: The True Nature of Time 41

THE INITIATIONS

THE FIRST INITIATION: Gateway Back to God 49

THE SECOND INITIATION: The Temple of Light 55

THE THIRD INITIATION: The Seed of Life 61

THE FOURTH INITIATION: The Power Flame 65

THE FIFTH INITIATION: The Shadow that Kept You Prisoner 71

THE SIXTH INITIATION: The Awakening of the Guru Within . . . 77

THE SEVENTH INITIATION: Your Body Is a Gateway into the
    Eternal Cosmos 81

THE EIGHTH INITIATION: The Turn of the Blue Key 85

THE NINTH INITIATION: The Paradigm of Love and Power 89

THE TENTH INITIATION: The Journey Back to Freedom and Sovereignty . . . 93

THE ELEVENTH INITIATION: The Gateway to Cosmic Consciousness 97

THE TWELFTH INITIATION: The Keepers of Divine Chance and Grace . . . 103

THE THIRTEENTH INITIATION: Step Into Mastery 109

THE FOURTEENTH INITIATION: The Power to Create 113

THE FIFTEENTH INITIATION: The Portal at the Back of Your Heart 117

THE SIXTEENTH INITIATION: Freedom from the Clock 119

THE SEVENTEENTH INITIATION: Becoming a Master Creator 123

THE EIGHTEENTH INITIATION: The Extraordinary One 127

THE NINETEENTH INITIATION: Of Blood and Soil 129

THE TWENTIETH INITIATION: Aurora 133

THE TWENTY-FIRST INITIATION: The Initiation of Father and Son 137

THE TWENTY-SECOND INITIATION: Make Way for God 141

THE TWENTY-THIRD INITIATION: Allow Yourself to Flourish 145

THE TWENTY-FOURTH INITIATION: Your Blessing from the Underworld . . . 149

THE TWENTY-FIFTH INITIATION: The Beauty of Two Worlds 153

THE TWENTY-SIXTH INITIATION: Everything in Good Time 157

THE TWENTY-SEVENTH INITIATION: All that You Are, and All that
You Are Yet to Become 161

THE TWENTY-EIGHTH INITIATION: Welcome to a New Beginning 167

The Galactic Army of Light: Who Are We, Where Are We? 173

The Crystalline Shield 175

From Here... 179

The Last Piece of the Puzzle 183

Dedicated to my angels, Lillian and Awen.
May you never forget.

Love Mummy

Free Deep Healing Meditation

DEEPLY HEAL ON ALL LEVELS AND BREAK THROUGH THE LIMITING VEILS OF SEPARATION

Your gift from Rhiannon

SCAN THE QR CODE OR GO TO GPRIESTESS.COM/GIFT TO ACCESS YOUR FREE MEDITATION

PREFACE

Beautiful reader, I am so delighted that this book has made its way into your hands! It truly is a collaboration and co-creation between myself and my team of divine guides. I want you to know that this book, although channeled, flows to you directly from my heart. I am with you as you read, and I am honoured by this opportunity to hold you and love you in the sacred container for transformation that is this text.

I want to share with you a little insight into who I am as the scribe and channel for this text, and how this book came to be.

I have always had an affinity for the mystical and magical. In fact, I have never felt truly and deeply connected to who I am in this human existence. I remember as a child having profound out-of-body experiences where I would feel deeply confused by my name, my body, and my very existence. I would look at my hands and ask myself, "Who am I?" And I would answer myself, "You are Rhiannon!" But that answer would only confuse me further, because then I would wonder, "… Who is Rhiannon?" Looking back, I now realise that as a child, I identified more deeply with my spirit self—my true self—than I did with my egoic identity of this lifetime. So, I have always been on the hunt for any experience or tool that allows me to soften my self of "I," my sense of "Rhiannon," and takes me back to the truth, where I know that I am infinitely more.

I was gifted my first set of oracle cards at age twenty-two, and from then onwards, I was hooked on all things mystical and magical. I longed to be in the otherworlds. I craved deep breath journeys, healing medicine journeys, and transcendent meditations. I felt as though I wanted to be anywhere but here, in my physical body, playing this role of "Rhiannon."

I spent much of my twenties as a yoga teacher. But my yoga classes focused more on esoteric teachings and pranayama than they did on asana, even when I was meant to be teaching power flow! The physical body has never held much meaning for me, nor has the emotional body. It is the energetic body and the spirit realms that have always guided my life, my focus, and my direction.

Around five years ago, I began to channel, writing in such a way that my mind was essentially switched off and my hand was on autopilot. Since then, I have never stopped channeling. As time has gone by, the magnitude of the messages coming through has intensified, becoming galactic in nature and intended for the entirety of humanity, rather than just for me.

In 2020, my team of guides told me that I would soon write a book that would need to be read by as many people as possible. Excited and curious, I kept trying to tune in and begin the process of channeling the book, but the words simply weren't ready to come through. I had to be patient—but more importantly, I needed to upgrade my own vibration in order to receive the words of this book. I now understand that I needed to ground, to integrate *life* as a spiritual practice. I needed to repair any separation that I had made between the magic realms and this Earth realm. And I needed first to truly understand that my daily life is the most magical and deeply spiritual practice I could ever find.

In September 2020, I became pregnant with our second baby girl. Chasing after a toddler while growing another baby in my belly was the quickest and toughest lesson in grounding into my humanity that I could imagine. I had no time to meditate, and I felt too nauseous to transcend my physical body. I was stuck in my day-to-day human life with nowhere to escape. So, I had to anchor the magical and mystical within my daily life. I had to ground and anchor my team of spirit guides into my physical realm. I learned to feel the Divine within me and all around me as I was chopping carrots in the kitchen. I learned to feel the devic kingdom and the fairy realm by gazing into the trees as I walked with my little one in the pram. I learned to feel God and see the angels as I stared up into the clouds while driving to buy groceries. And all of a sudden, I realised that true and integrated spirituality wasn't about leaving my body and venturing into the cosmos. True and integrated spirituality comes from being so deeply connected to the absolute bliss of the present that all space and time can be accessed in every NOW moment without ever even needing to close your eyes.

This was the lesson that I needed to integrate before I could attune to and channel the words of this text. This book, *The Keepers of the Light Codes*, is that initiation and that lesson. Through a series of practices and lessons, this book activates and alchemizes the part of you that knows God in every moment. This book and these practices are here to bring online the part of you that can venture infinitely into time and space with your eyes closed, and yet can also venture infinitely into bliss and ecstasy through a sip of your morning coffee. There is no separation; it is all God, and this book is here to remind us of that.

For so many of us, spirituality has been a journey of seeking—a neverending series of healings, retreats, meditations, realisations, workshops, teachers, gurus, books, and more. So many of us on the path to ascension have been looking to uncover our unloved aspects so that we can heal, grow, and expand. The spiritual journey for many of us has been cyclical, a wheel of suffering, healing, expansion, and more suffering. This book is here to tell you that this cycle can end here. It no longer serves you, and you are now ready to move into your enlightenment. You are ready to claim your status as a master and release any idea that you are not divinity and pure realised perfection as you are right now.

This book has found its way into your loving hands, and therefore, a few assumptions can be made about where you are in your ascension at this moment in time. Your resonance with these words means that you have healed in this lifetime more deeply and completely than you can possibly imagine. You already see through the veils of the 3D matrix. You already identify as the soul that you are. You are not a beginner in these teachings, and therefore, this text will not speak to you as a beginner. This text will speak to you as the master that you are, ready to be realised and activated so that you can experience God and the Divine in every single waking moment of your beautiful existence.

Before my pregnancy with my second baby girl, Awen May, I would spend hours meditating and channeling in a candlelit room, surrounded by crystals and trinkets on my perfectly arranged altar. Channeling this book has looked rather different. With no time for such indulgences around my meditation practice, much of this book was actually channeled and written on my phone while I was parked in a carpark with a sleeping toddler and newborn in the back seat. I have learned that connection to my spirit guides just *is*. They are not waiting for me to light a candle in order to come through. Spirit is simply waiting for my pure presence. Pure presence is true mastery, and pure presence can be found in the most mundane moments of day-to-day life. This means that the ultimate spiritual practice occurs in pure presence, in loving the mundane moments of life and thus transforming mundane into magic, boring into bliss.

✳

Meditation has always been a sacred tool for me. I have always used and still use meditation to connect to other realms, places, and times outside of this perceived reality. Meditation allows us to make contact and connect with all that exists beyond this 3D reality. This text will initiate within you the ability to make contact and connection with such realms. But this text will also initiate within you the energy needed to ground these divine connections into your current reality, making your day-to-day life infinitely more expansive and divinely inspired. This text will initiate and alchemise within you your ability to hold the light of the Divine in every moment, making you a sacred antenna for galactic and interdimensional connection and guidance.

You will be upgraded by reading this text. You have done so much work on yourself to be who you are, and now this text has found you at the perfect time. You are ready to truly integrate, once and for all, the purest aspect of your spirituality with all that you are in your entirety.

I have channeled this book at this moment in time because this is when it is absolutely needed by humanity. As a collective, we are experiencing a vibrational upgrade unlike ever before. These channeled words will assist you in this upgrade. They will alchemise you to hold and ground more light—the light of God—so that you can assist in collectively anchoring Heaven on Earth.

I have channeled this book through my team of trusted spirit guides. This team will reveal itself to you at the end of the book, but for now, know that this team is a collective consciousness of light beings from across the cosmos, through infinite dimensions, and through timelines past, present, and future.

I have enjoyed every moment of channeling this book! It has flowed through me with so much ease, and the words have taught me so much. Each lesson and initiation that has come through has initiated me in the same way that it will initiate you. I have been activated by these words, and so too will you be. Follow the guidance within the pages, and allow Spirit to talk to you and lead you through the teachings and practices that lie ahead. The lessons and initiations are a final boot camp for you in your ascension, if you will. You will be pushed to open, purge, and expand, and you will be initiated through the words and the practices into your mastery. Trust that you are ready for this. Trust that you are ready to activate all of your light, all of your power, and all of your love. Trust that you are ready to integrate pure divinity into your day-to-day existence, so that you can serve as an anchor point for Heaven on Earth.

As an intuitive, I know who is finding this book and aligning with these words. I know that your heart is opening with excitement and apprehension at this moment. You are ready to move beyond all doubts and all veils of illusion that are keeping you from living a life of pure God-inspired bliss.

Be ready now, beautiful friend, and I will feel you and see you on the other side of your sacred initiation into being a keeper of the light codes.

THE KEEPERS OF
THE LIGHT CODES

Who are the keepers of the light codes? They are strong, they are wise, they are knowing, and they are unwavering in their commitment to God, to truth, and to the Light Divine. The keepers are not ones who are flawless, but rather, ones who seek to see that which they can understand better, delve into, transcend, and transform. These are the codes and the wisdom that seek to initiate the keeper within you—the keeper that is already you.

From this day on, you will understand better. From this day on, you will know more deeply. From this day, your initiation begins. This book will teach you and train you to hold the light that is yours to hold. This book will ask you to peel back layers and veils that are holding you trapped in a false way of being, a false light. This book will seek to show you yourself, and as you are revealed to you, you will uncover your truth and your mastery. This book is the start of something great for you, and that is your true coming home, the final leg of the long journey back to the temple of your heart.

You have done so much to be here, and now here you sit, ready to embark on this final leg of the journey. Your ascension is not yet complete, but it will be soon—and when it is, light will stream through you and anchor you as a portal yourself between sun and stars, God and Earth, Earth and the Infinite. You have been given this message because you are ready now to initiate. You are ready to hold the light of the Divine within you. You are ready to shine as a beacon of God on planet Earth. And when you do, you will laugh and smile, because from that moment onwards, the journey ends, the quest stops, and you experience Heaven on Earth as a single moment in time, limitlessly full of God's perfection. From then onwards, there is nothing to do. From then onwards, there is no one to become. You are it, because you have remembered that which you always were: a keeper of the light codes, ready to hold God's grace and glory in every cell, in every fibre of your being, in every moment.

To hold this, you must upgrade. Of course, you can hold this now, because that is the true nature of your crystalline DNA fabric. But you don't—not yet. And why is that? Because you have not been ready. You have needed to suffer through life's first initiations to be where you are now. You have needed to journey to this level of mastery before you could attune to these words. You have needed to shed, to purge, and to burn the perils of past lives and ancestral trauma. And now you have, and now you are ready for the final leg of the journey, the last initiation into mastery, into being a true keeper of the light codes.

With that, we welcome you. You have not come this far to be shown the journey back to suffering. You have come this far to transcend, once and for all, that which no longer serves you. Suffering may have served you once, but now, no longer, for you are ready to upgrade to a level of mastery whereby you see, witness, feel, heal, and transcend all within a flickering moment in the matrix. For you are ready to transcend space and time, and the notion of suffering that is embedded within it. Nothing needs to be worked through over days, months, or years. The present moment is enough for the keepers of the light codes. In the present moment, an intention meets God's grace, and in that, the work is done; all is healed. No hurdle cannot be climbed, no obstacle is too great in the quantum space of light. All is done, all is healed within a flicker of light in a moment in time. This is the reality of where you are heading.

Ascension is a journey. You are heading into a time where your ascension is done; *it is*, and therefore, *you are*. There will be nowhere to go other than home in each moment, back to the crystalline fibres of that which you are, and no further, for those crystalline fibres are the gateway to infinity, and you can access that in an instant. This is your rite of passage now. This is where you are journeying to on the sacred final leg of your travels.

You are a warrior of light at present, fighting to remember, battling to know your truth and the truth of God. You have been fighting for your light for so long, journeying uphill to purge, to let go, to heal, and to remember. Now you have arrived, and it is time to drink from the golden chalice of the Temple of Light. It is time to receive your final initiation and put down your sword. You have made it, dear one. You are ready to hold the sacred codes that anoint you into your truth as a realised master of the light worlds. You are ready to claim your throne as a light being of Heaven on Earth, here to serve and love with pure thought and intention.

You have to step up now and rise to the task. Your role as victim ends here. Your role in the spiritual quest ends here. Your role as the seeker ends here. You are none of these things now. You are done. You are transitioning now from warrior of light into keeper of the light codes. The keeper has it all, and therefore, there is now nothing to fight for, to strive for, or to journey to. You are done—and when you realise that you are done, truly, your initiation is complete.

Come with us now, into the final leg of your journey. Come with us as the keeper that you already are. Come with us with the knowing that you are complete, ascended, and perfectly divine, and let every lesson anchor that knowing into your absolute realisation and liberation.

This is the time, and we love you.

THE LESSONS

These lessons are the start of your initiation into being a keeper of the light codes. These lessons need to be read to allow the imprint on your DNA fabric to occur. These lessons are activating and will bring online the dormant DNA strands that hold your ability to remember and know the light being that you already are. Once you are activated in this way, these lessons will hold no significance for you, for they are not needed; your divine memory has already been triggered. These lessons will allow you to see yourself differently, as a complete and whole aspect of the Divine, and from there, your final initiation will be well and truly underway.

You may choose to have these lessons read to you while you lie or sit in rest. The activating nature of these lessons holds a vibration, and that vibration is best received from a space of passive receptivity. Therefore, if you work in service as a healer and hold the intention to activate humanity into their remembering, these lessons should be read to those who come for your services. The power of the words in these upcoming lessons is rewiring and activating and will enhance significantly the divine intention of remembering, whether that intention is set for yourself or for another.

The words within these lessons need to be understood in a way that perhaps understanding has never taken place for you before. To understand truly is to feel the essence of the words as a vibration—a vibration that massages the fabric of who you are. And with that intention, it is so.

Allow your heart to open as you dive forward into these lessons. We welcome you to your great remembering, the start of your great activation, your initiation into being a keeper of the light codes.

THE FABRIC OF
WHO YOU ARE

The fabric of who you are is not mere flesh and bones. You are crystalline in nature. You have been reduced to physical matter through the limited perception that you have held. You have seen in the mirror your physical body, and from the belief that your five senses are the only senses, you have previously concluded that your physical body is your only body. That which you can see with your two eyes and touch with your two hands is who you are. You have been bound by the limitations of your physical body from the perception that that is who you are. You have only been able to travel as far as your body will carry you, and you have only been able to see as far as your eyes can look into the distance.

Can you stare into the mirror and cast your eyes through and beyond the physical body that you see? Can you stare through and beyond detail and into light, shadow, and vibration? Your body is a hologram; what exists beyond that hologram?

Can you sit with yourself before a mirror and ask the mirror to show you, *Who am I?* Can you stare a vacant stare that seeks to see nothing, and with that, see an aspect that you have never seen before?

You are not that body, and so, who are you?

You are the Light Divine. Your body is but a hologram in time.

And through your vacant stare into the mirror of limitless perceptions, start to chant and repeat, "I am the Light Divine; show me beyond this mirror in time."

What does the mirror show you? When you close your eyes, what does your internal mirror show you?

LET THERE BE LIGHT
IN YOUR HEART

et there be light in your heart and truth in your eyes. You are a beacon for divine wisdom, and it is time for you to know that. When we ask you to open your heart, do it from a place of love. Do it from a place of remembering that feeling that cracks you open to beauty, purity, and simplicity.

The heart can never be accessed via the mind. You cannot think to be in the heart and be there. You must arrive by a feeling, a journeying through the fabric of love. Until you remember love in any given moment, you cannot access the space of your heart. The heart is a temple, and it has a doorway. That doorway leads you to all things, all manner of knowing. Until you arrive at this temple, you will be lost and confused. Until you remember love as a feeling and not a thought, that doorway to the temple of the heart will remain closed.

We have to tell you this now. So many know that the heart holds all secrets, and through that knowing, they seek to enter the heart. But their thoughts lead them astray, for the heart cannot be accessed through a knowing of the mind; it MUST always be accessed through feeling, through a remembering of love. This is a wisdom that has been taught, but also forgotten. So many have led others to the heart through the doorway of the mind, and there has been no magic, no mystery to be revealed, for it was never the heart that was being accessed.

The heart beckons you now. It summons you to enter the sacred temple of all wisdom, all space, and all time. This is your right and this is your privilege as a sacred being of this holy land. So, now we ask you to go there. Go to the heart. Enter the heart's temple through the doorway of love and nothing else. Breathe into love at this temple centre as you never have before. Focus on love as a feeling, until the doorway swings open and sweeps you into the temple of light that has lain dormant, waiting to be reopened.

Let this be a truth that you never forget. You must feel love at your heart in every moment in order to be connected to the Light Divine. When love leaves, you lose access to the temple of the heart, and you lose resonance with God, who seeks to support you and love you in every moment.

This love that you feel at the heart may not always be pretty. Love of your rage, love of your sadness, love of your joy, love of your peace: these are all loves. With love comes acceptance and a vibrational attunement to God. And from that attunement, you are at peace, at one with the infinite present moment—and from there, there can be no true sorrow.

You are ready to take this step. Allow yourself to feel more love now than you ever have. Breathe into your heart in such a way that love overcomes you—love for all things. Allow this love to sweep over you as a wave of energy and invite you into the doorway of your heart, where you will receive this initiation into the temple centre of all remembering.

Welcome home.

OPEN YOUR
HEART TO LOVE

Open your heart to love and allow love to shower in. This is the key to all things. This love that is waiting to emanate down on you will change you and move you back to God. You have to understand what is meant by this, and we will share this with you now.

Your heart is a capacitor, capable of receiving universal and galactic intelligence in the form of knowing, wisdom, truth, and love. Your heart is an antenna, a radar device that can beam light into the cosmos and thus receive infinitely from the cosmos that which is resonant and required. This ability is nothing short of extraordinary, and yet it is yours to be reclaimed and to be utilised in all moments throughout this lifetime and beyond. Your ability to open and receive through the portal of the heart is your birthright and your gift, and thus you will be led to this remembering an untold number of times until this message is heard, understood, and integrated. One such moment is now.

Your heart is going to begin to receive now, quantumly and infinitely, all manner of wisdom, knowledge, and love from galactic sources far and wide. You will start to attune to more wisdom than you have ever known. Why? Because the temple of your heart has been activated. Because the beam of cosmic light that emanates from your heart is ready to be received as a beacon by the cosmos. And thus, from there, YOU are ready to receive back into your heart infinite love, wisdom, and truth, felt as the vibration of loving perfection in this God-given moment.

This is why your heart must be open. Yes, to feel; yes, to love; yes, to trust; but especially to reactivate the cosmic connection of the open temple of the heart with the Infinite.

We have guided you to this reading now to show you and remind you of the power that you hold. You are no longer to be kept small or separate, for you are neither of those things. You are infinite power, wisdom, love, and trust. You are the galactic space of infinity. You are whatever you need, whatever you want, whatever you command. You are the cosmic light of intelligence. You are the power centre of the universe. Where? At your heart—at your fully activated, opened, and aligned temple centre of the heart.

THE GATEWAY TO GOD

The gateway to God, as you know, is the heart. And yet it is more than just the heart alone. Once the heart has been activated, the gateway to God widens to become all things. This is the first understanding of the infinite nature of all things, for the heart centre, as a standalone point in space, holds in itself a notion of separation—a notion that one place, one space, one energy is separate from all else. Any notion of separation is never truth. Let us explain.

The heart holds an energy, a vibration, and this energy can be felt, beamed, and resonated into all things beyond the fabric of space and time. Once the heart has been activated, this energy can be felt and harnessed anywhere.

Once the heart knows how to feel infinite connection with Source, the same can be experienced within the fingers or the toes. When the heart truly activates, it sets off an electromagnetic boom that supercharges every aspect of your being with the wisdom and magic of the temple centre of the heart. This is what it means to be truly open to God.

The heart is the gateway to God, and yet once that gateway is opened, *all* of you is a gateway to God. From a moment of quiet feeling and soft intention, any space within you can be activated and aligned to the frequency of the cosmos to receive and communicate at the vibration of infinite love and wisdom. This is the cosmic reality of what it means to be in true unity—that is, unity with all of your being vibrating at the energy of the activated heart; that is, unity with all of the cosmos communicating and connecting with all of you at the vibration of your activated heart. This is the magic of what it means to be human.

Your body is a sacred antenna. Your body is a vessel of God. Your body is a portal to the cosmos. All of you can open to give and receive at the vibration of the Light Divine, but only when you are activated at the heart. The heart is the sacred antenna to universal wisdom and connection, and once this antenna is tuned in and turned on, YOU are the sacred antenna. You are the beacon of light that streams forth and radiates love infinitely upward and outward. You, activated at your heart, shine light in every cell of your being, and this light allows all of you to be seen and loved from the farthest corners of the galactic. Yes, your heart is the first sacred gateway to God, but once activated, YOU in your physical and energetic entirety are the gateway, doorway, portal, and antenna to God, the Infinite, all of space, and all of time.

You are ready now to know this and feel this.

Close your eyes.

Your heart is open.

Breathe into love at your heart like never before.

Breathe into your activated and aligned temple centre of the heart.

Feel love emanate from you.

Feel the love you hold for the cosmos in your heart.

Feel the connection you hold to the cosmos in your heart.

Feel that connection now in all of your body, in all of your being.

Feel the infinite space of the cosmos in and around your legs.

Feel the infinite space of the cosmos in and around your spine.

Feel the infinite space of the cosmos in and around your head and crown.

Feel the infinite space of the cosmos in and around your entire body.

You are that.

You are the infinite wisdom of all of space, and you are ready to hold that now in your body.

THE LIBERATION
OF SELF

To realise that you yourself are a portal to God and the Infinite is to lose your sense of self altogether, for if you are a beacon of light communicating with and connecting to all things, then you yourself are an aspect of all things. To know this is to know God, for in losing yourself and the concept of separation, you become the infinite plane of existence that is the Light Divine manifesting as all things. When this understanding is integrated, the path to absolute liberation has begun. We want to guide you down this path now.

This path to liberation starts with this: the understanding that you are a portal to the cosmos, and thus you are the cosmos in and amongst itself. Just as you can feel the stars and the galactic in your toes, your toes are the stars and the galactic. And so, who are you? You are all of space. You are all things and all time expressing itself as you. And your "youness" is simply that—nothing more than an expression, no more meaningful or permanent than an expression on your face.

"You," as you have always perceived yourself to be, is a character, an illusion, a construct. So then, we ask you this: who are you really? Are you the infinite cosmos that you feel in your fingers and toes? Or is that too merely an illusion? When you dissolve all constructs of the *you* that you could be, what is left? What is left is a seed of light with infinite potential. That seed is as little and meaningless as one could imagine, and yet as infinitely significant as all of space. You are that seed of light, and that seed of light is God. This is to know God, and this is to liberate yourself from the idea that God is separate from you.

Now do you see? The idea of your connection to spirit has nothing to do with the embellishments of the illusion of self. Nothing to do with the meditation, the practice, the mantra. Nothing to do with the clothing, the adornments, the gurus, or the icons. Connection to spirit or the spiritual is simply connection to God. And connection to God is the knowing that within you lies a seed of light, and that seed is all that you are and all that you have ever been. That seed is the infinite cosmos, the soil, the sea, and the sand. That seed of light can never be replaced or destroyed; it just is, and you are that and only that. All else beyond the knowing of that seed of light is a meaningless illusion that is there to play with, to enjoy, and to dance in. But to believe that that dance is anything more than an illusion is to forget God in that moment.

THE START OF
THE NEXT CHAPTER

And so, you have freed yourself from the illusory construct of your false identity. You have made peace with your nothingness and your wholeness. What is next? You lose yourself in life. You lose yourself in the game of life as though it is a play, a pantomime, there to tantalise and delight your senses. The play itself—that is, your life—is an illusion like all else, constructed and created by the perceptions of your mind, so why shouldn't the play be spectacular? Why shouldn't your illusory existence be extraordinary? It should be. Why? Because you simply decide in any given moment whether your life will be extraordinary or not—and why would you choose the latter?

This is the impermanence of the game of life. Nothing should be focused on or felt as real other than the love in your heart that connects you to the truth of your existence. All else is not real. It is pretend. It is a dream. And that dream is constructed by the thoughts of your mind and your interpretation of light as a holographic reality.

We want to explain to you something so simple now.

Let go. Let go and enjoy. You do not need to fight or force or try. Allow your life to just be, knowing that as the quality of the light you hold increases, so too does the quality of the holographic reality of your existence. There is nothing that you can create from force alone. Creation, for you, now begins through your communication with the Infinite. Start to receive messages from the Light Divine, and allow these messages to guide you and flow you into your most glorious expression of life. These messages will support you and uplift you every day from here on in.

You have a job to do, and that job, no matter how big or small, is divine. That job is to receive light codes, and to allow these light codes to be the substance and fabric of your existence. How do you receive these light codes? By activating the temple centre of your heart through love, by feeling your connection to the Infinite as a beam of light that streams forth from your heart to all of space, and by allowing yourself to feel and notice your connection to the Light Divine in every aspect of your being. In doing this, you are receiving light codes. You are receiving guidance for how to flow and move forward with your life experience.

Yes, your life experience is a dream, an illusion. However, it serves a purpose, and that purpose is to enliven and enrich all beings from their dream state and into the interconnected, intergalactic true nature of reality.

How do you best act out this purpose? By opening, by letting go, and by dancing through life as a natural and fully activated conduit for the Light Divine. How *you* acting out this purpose should look is of no importance and no meaning. The dance of life should feel electric, and that is the true indicator of alignment with this purpose. There is no other measurable parameter of alignment to purpose other than the ecstatic glow of love and aliveness that can be felt in the body and the heart.

So, isn't this the lesson that offers a conundrum? It is the conundrum of knowing that you have a purpose here on this Earth, and yet the only action required to fulfill that purpose is whatever leads you to joy, love, and ecstasy. If you follow this blueprint, then by natural and organic order, you assist with the activation of a sleeping humanity, and that humanity's realisation and remembering of the divine nature of all things. There is nothing more to do than that!

All steps, roads, and pathways that lead to love, joy, and ecstasy must be fulfilled. When you are activated at the heart, you will know and be shown these pathways *always*, and with absolute clarity.

And so, with that, can you relax? Can you remove the pressure that you have placed upon yourself? Can you stop measuring yourself in dollars and time, and rather in joy and love? How perfect could you be to yourself if you allowed yourself to accept the ease that is available to you right now? Choose this now. This is the path ahead from here: no fighting, no forcing, only allowing the dance of life to flow through you in the direction of the Light Divine, measured by love, joy, and ecstasy only.

The ease of life was always meant to be felt by all beings. The hardship of life is an illusion and a trap. It is not real, and it is something that you can choose to disconnect with now. Hardship is not truth. When you are open and activated at the heart, you are always led and guided to light. Nothing works against you, but rather for you. The dance of life is divine, and it is yours to enjoy now.

THE SATISFACTION
OF KNOWING

The satisfaction of knowing is just that: the absolute satisfaction and pleasure in knowing that all is perfect and all is fine. Because you are a keeper of the light codes, nothing is ever out of place or out of alignment. Why? Because in imperfection, there is always perfection. Because in pain, there is never suffering. Because in drama, there is always an observer. And because in chaos, there is always a divine rearrangement. And in that knowing, there is absolute peace—that is, absolute peace in all things, in all moments in time.

We want you to see and feel the perfection now of all things. Nothing is exempt from this law of truth. All things, people, places, and events are always expressing themselves as they were intended to. Nothing is breaking from the plan. Nothing is unruly or without correct divine direction. All things are playing out perfectly according to the Divine Matrix.

And with that, can you simply watch without judgment? Can you simply know with absolute satisfaction? *It* always needs to be exactly as *it* is. *It* always needs to go through the exact process of correction and redirection. With that, can you know that there is never anything to fix or change or redirect? All things, places, events, and people are on their perfect trajectory, and there is never anything for you to do. Your light and your natural path of joy, love, and ecstasy may appear to redirect or shift the direction of certain people, places, or things, but this was always in the divine trajectory of the movement of all things.

With that, you can watch and witness everything and everyone with no judgment. They are doing and acting and moving in flow with the Divine, always. How that flow looks to you is not your concern. Witness that flow without judgment, and with love, and with the satisfaction of knowing that all things move in absolute perfection, with no exceptions. With that, welcome to peace, and welcome to the satisfaction of knowing.

THE ART OF LETTING GO

When you come to remember that everything is as it is and as it ought to be, nothing is worth holding onto emotionally, mentally, or energetically. All must flow. Just as life itself is a beautiful journey of waves rising and retreating, the emotional body is a space that also should be transient and impermanent. To hold onto that which doesn't serve is to cast darkness into an internal space that could be filled with light. To hold onto a thought, a memory, or a feeling is to cling to a paradigm that doesn't exist, rather than opening to the infinite expansiveness of all that could be in any moment. We want you to know this because so many of your people seek to know truth and light and fail to understand the darkness that comes with their attachment to their memory, mind, and emotions.

The memory is a storage vault of ideas. These ideas are limited in nature. These ideas are simply pictures of a fixed and outdated reality. Memory is like a film; it is one fixed and limited story, and if one were to watch the same film over and over again, one would never expand, never learn, and never grow. To look to the memory to give meaning to the present is to decipher a glorious and unknown space of potential from the wisdom obtained from an old and outdated movie. This will never allow for a deep understanding of the present moment or life itself, but rather, this will result in the exact same limited interpretation of every possible situation or experience.

Life could be infinitely glorious, and yet, when experienced by a mind fixated on memories of the past, life will only ever be perceived from the learned ideas of those memories. These ideas need to be let go of. These memories need to be released. They are not worthy of revisiting. They hold no substance or value. All that truly needs to be learned and integrated has been already, and thus the memory itself is of no service to you and your expansion.

Stop revisiting your memories. They mean nothing now. And the stories that you are telling yourself and creating as a result of constant revisitation are holding you back and keeping you captive in a way of being that is not your full potential. Cast your vision into the future, and never the past. The future holds the vibration of infinite potential. The future can be felt, seen, and understood through the heart and lived, in its fullest expression, in the present moment. Why? Because time doesn't exist. Time is not linear. You can access your past and your future now. So why access the limited and restricting nature of your past now, when you could be accessing the vibration of your divine and magical future now?

Do you see what we are saying? Let go of the past. It is of no value to you. Let go of the emotions that come from the mind frequently revisiting the past. These emotions are not real, and they are weighing you down. What happened yesterday, last week, last year, or last decade is of no consequence. The *now* moment is the only moment worthy of your focus, and from this *now* moment, you can create and cast anything into the future. You need to know and understand this simple rule of the nature of time and all things. Time is elastic and not linear. If you hold onto a fixed idea, you then cast time into a fixed trajectory. Let go of all fixed ideas such as memories, and allow the true nature of time to be felt in the present moment.

THE TRUE
NATURE OF TIME

The true nature of time needs to be felt to be understood. Once you have completed this lesson, you will start to feel and understand time in all its expansiveness and elasticity.

Time is not as you have understood it. Time is not as you have read on a clock or a calendar. Time is far deeper than these constructs would ever allow you to interpret. We want you to try to understand the true nature of time, so that you can see how little value your clock or calendar holds.

All of time starts now. This *now* moment is the beginning of time, and all extends from here. Time allows us to fold inward to see all aspects of ourselves now. Time allows us to fold outwards to see all truths of the universe now. Time reverses, fast-forwards, retracts, and unwinds constantly, and with that, time is never the same. A single second can never be measured, because the nature of reality is multidimensional and moving differently depending on where you stand in any moment in the multidimensional truth of reality.

Time is layered. It moves quickly and slowly at the same time, depending on your perception and vibration. You navigate your entire existence in the present moment only. So, you only ever experience the beginning of time, and with that, you only ever truly experience a moment in time that is bathed in the field of infinite potential.

If we have lost you, that is ok. These words are here to be read and will be understood when and only when the true nature of time has been felt and integrated. For now, we want you to sit with this idea…

To let go is to move on.

To wish away is to cast backwards.

To cultivate is to draw towards you that which is ahead of you.

To smile is to bend your energy into a new frequency for a new beginning of time.

To release is to move away from and sail forward.

You are ready to see and feel this truth as we cast you into this new way of being where nothing holds permanence or lasting significance.

THE
INITIATIONS

W e want you to see now what you have to do in order to call in a new way of being. A new way of being awaits you—one where you are totally liberated and free from all limitations of the mind, the ego, and the past.

You have to see that your job starts now. You need to step into your vibrational perfection and meet the resonance of God. God awaits you, and God's glory is here for you to be felt now. Your journey back to wholeness is nearly at fruition. Well done! We commend you for all that you have done so far in order to be here, resonating with and hearing these words. These words will only speak to you when you have come to your final stage of initiation—that is, when you are ready to step out of the cycle of suffering > reflection > expansion > suffering and into your liberation and freedom as a keeper of the light codes, whereby all is felt, loved, and integrated in a single moment in time with God's grace. This is your final initiation, and from here on in, you are truly free—not free of work or effort, but free from burden, suffering, and searching.

We have for you now a series of smaller initiations to complete and

integrate this overall initiation that welcomes you into your vibration as a keeper of the light codes. These smaller initiations are layered and multidimensional in nature. These initiations will speak to
you on a soul level and will invite you to purge any baggage, chains,
cords, or shackles that bind you to old ways of being and lower fre-
quencies. The smaller initiations that lie ahead within this text are
infinitely powerful and can be revisited randomly upon the systematic completion of all initiations, which should be completed in order,
one through twenty-eight initially.

As you move through these initiations, you will start to notice shifts
in your energy body. You will start to perceive the world and your
life differently. You will start to change in your desires, wants, and
needs. You will move into a new vibrational frequency that is resonant with different people, places, and experiences, and with that,
your life will change. You will have many experiences as you move
through these initiations. Some will feel meaningless and of no value,
and others will feel significant and poignant. How you interpret your
experience of each initiation is of no significance, for the magic and
potion is in the systematic doing and completion of all initiations
and not in the analysis of each one.

When you have completed the final initiation, number twenty-eight,
you have arrived, and you are a keeper of the light codes. You will
hold all that we have discussed and mentioned and more. And with
that, you will be free and liberated from everything that is not God,
that is not love. Why? Because that is the power that the keepers
hold and the choice that they can make in any moment—that is, the
choice to come back to God and love no matter what.

These initiations work with layers of the subconscious, ancestral lin-
eage conditioning, past life patterning and programming, artificial
intelligence and dark agenda infiltration, weaponization of the astral
space, and infinitely more. These initiations invite back memories on
a soul level of intergalactic belonging and wisdom. These initiations

are not to be taken lightly, for although they are here to bring you back fully into your light body, they do so by accessing and transmuting all that is not that. These initiations will involve an energetic purge like never before. This purge will occur multidimensionally and not just in the physical and emotional body. With each purge comes an expansion, and with each aspect of the dark self that is accessed, a new level of light is accessed. It is from the light that true magic arises—the magic of God, the magic of love, the magic of bliss and ecstasy. The duality of darkness only exists for us to better understand the light, for the light is where your true human potential exists. So, this is a journey into light—not through the idea that the dark is to be avoided or bypassed, but through the knowing that the aspects of self that are dark need to be journeyed into and loved into bliss in order for more light to be held.

So, be prepared, for these initiations will ask you to meet yourself fully as the soul spark of the Divine that you are, in all of your perfection and imperfection, in all of your permanence and impermanence, in all of your glory and greatness, weakness and patheticness. You are a child of God, and all of you is divine. And in your journey back to light and wholeness, you will remember that truth. You are a shining light of the Infinite, and you are ready to peel back the layers that you don't yet know exist in order to revel in the absolute ecstasy that is your fully realised God self experiencing human existence.

Come with us, and let it begin now.

GATEWAY BACK
TO GOD

The gateway to God is a chamber that exists within the heart. This chamber can be accessed and activated at any time, but only when the individual is ready, having understood and integrated the importance and meaning of a true heart connection.

The gateway to God exists as a chamber, and this chamber is not physical in nature. This chamber is an energetic dimension that is a portal and gateway to all of eternity and all of infinity. This chamber, once accessed, is infinity in itself, and therefore is the gateway to all things—all manner of time, space, and knowing.

To access this chamber of the heart is to unlock the portal that connects you to all things. That which we call "God" *is* all things, as "God" is simply a term for the wisdom and perfection of all of infinity and eternity. To access this chamber is to enter the realm of infinite possibility, infinite creativity, and infinite divine wisdom. This chamber is the portal to everything, as it is in itself everything!

Once you obtain and unlock access to the sacred chamber of your heart, you begin to live your life as a fully realised and expressed divine human being, who is creative beyond measure, and who holds secrets of God too profoundly wonderful to reduce to words! This secret—the secret chamber of the heart—is ready to be shared with you now. You are ready to unlock and access the chamber of your heart to truly know God—that is, the God within, the God that you are, the infinite nature of all of creation that you are.

This energetic chamber of the heart can be visualised and understood as a cave—that is, a dark cavernous space that exists within the internal space of your chest. To understand and follow the practice for this initiation, you must try to visualise a black cave at the centre of your chest. This black cave may appear to you as a dark opening within a rock formation. Can you try to bring all of your awareness to your heart centre, and then visualise a dark cave? It is this dark cavernous space that, once entered, expands to all of infinity. This is the chamber of God. This is the chamber of all knowing wisdom. The black nature of the cave space allows for you to then feel how infinitely outwardly expansive the space is, into the blackness of the cosmos and beyond. This black space is truly the portal to God, the portal to the Light Divine, and it lives within your beautiful chest.

YOU ARE READY NOW TO BEGIN THE INITIATION PRACTICE.

This initiation practice includes visualisation, spoken prayer, and toning. Follow these steps to complete this first initiation: Gateway Back to God.

This initiation must be carried out in one uninterrupted sitting. All steps to this practice must be completed systematically, without any omissions or amendments. Ensure this initiation is completed in a sacred and quiet space, free from any disruption, and with reverence.

This initiation may be completed as either a self-practice, or as a guided practice whereby the receiver of the initiation is led passively through an internal journey by another. Either way is sufficient; however, in the case of a self-led practice, ensure that the entire process is read and understood before commencement to ensure that the energy created throughout the process is not broken when instructional points are read. You may also choose to record yourself reading the initiation to follow along with later, making sure to allow time to perform each step as instructed.

1. Lie down in a quiet space. Breathe into the body. Breathe into the heart. Allow the mind to be absorbed by the breath at the feeling heart.

2. Once anchored in the heart, read these words, and allow them to be felt as a transmission from the Divine:

   "The gateway back to God is open for you. Come with us now, and let us show you God's grace. You are ready to be opened and anointed fully into your sacred perfection. You are ready for this catalyst, this change, this monumental moment in time."

3. You are now ready to be fully opened at the heart. Slowly place your flat and open hand over your heart as you breathe into and maintain connection with the heart centre.

4. Read these words as a transmission from the Divine:

   "We ask God's grace to come forward now, to open this pure heart back to the perfection of love."

5. Follow this visualisation process as you breathe into the energy at your heart centre:

- See the internal black cave of the heart that lives within your chest.

- We ask this internal cave of the heart to expand and widen.

- See how infinitely it can grow. From the small and humble dark cave that you see now, open and grow this cave infinitely within the heart space.

- Now watch and feel this dark cave grow infinitely bigger and wider, until the dark space within the heart is the infinite cosmos expanding into all that is.

- This is your heart, and this is your gateway to God.

- Let light into your heart now. This blackness was merely here to show you the Infinite that lies within. The truth of this space is flickering white light in nature.

- See all of space, all of infinity, as flickering white light existing from your heart.

- Om Tat Sat, and so it is.

6. This vibration that has been accessed within the heart holds a sacred resonance. You must attune to this resonance through sound, through song. This song must be sung from the heart. This tone is the sound of the eternal light that echoes from the heart chamber. With the eyes still closed, sing this chant and bathe in the vibration of "heeee" as sung from the open and realised heart.

> *"Heeeeeeeeeeeee*
> *Heeeee heeeeeee*

Heeeeeeeeeeee
Heeeee heeeeee
Heeeeeeeeeeee
Heeeee heeeeee"

7. The heart can be massaged through this toning process. Keeping your flat and open hand on your heart, very softly but quickly vibrate the hand. This will further open the heart space to feel the resonance of the infinite cosmic light.

8. Rest completely for ten minutes or more to feel the effects of this initiation. In the case of a self-practice, the initiation may need to be repeated immediately in order to dive deeper into the practice without the distraction of the mind learning and following the instructions. The first attempt can be viewed as a practice run or rehearsal needed to integrate and learn the process before the main event.

THE TEMPLE
OF LIGHT

The holy grail of the human existence is the temple of light. The temple of light is the ecstasy and bliss realm that can be felt at any given moment in time. The temple of light is a dimension that one may enter through higher states of being, such as ecstatic liberation and bliss. To arrive at the temple of light is to arrive at human potential, fully realised and activated.

The temple of light, as an energy, may be felt and accessed for a short, fleeting second, or lived in and danced in day after day. But know that once the temple of light has been accessed, divine permission has then been granted for return at any time, for any duration of stay. The temple of light is a state of being that is the ultimate state of being for the human being. It is God consciousness felt within the ecstasy of the human experience. It is God consciousness, bliss, and euphoria, felt within a dance, a deep communion with nature, an intimate sacred union with a beloved, a windswept moment of earthly energetic delight. The human activity that transcends you into the temple of light is not important, but once you have entered the heavenly state of being that is orgasmic ecstasy held by the love of God, it will never be forgotten.

You can enter this temple of light now, purely through your intention and the invitation for this energy to initiate within you. Once this energy has been activated, you are thereby granted lifelong access to the temple of light, on demand, by you, at will. Take yourself there now through this initiation, and you can take yourself there over and over again. You can uplift now to this temple of light energy, the dimension of love, ecstasy, and bliss. You can activate this energy now to experience the potency of what it truly means to be human. Then you can revisit this energy throughout your day, throughout your life, in the magic moments of the mundane that are the temple of light.

WELCOME NOW TO THE
SECOND INITIATION PRACTICE.

This is the practice where you will feel God in your groin, in your heart, and in your hands. Then, through the movement of your divinely activated body, you will make love to the magic of life that exists all around you. This is to know God in your ecstasy, to know God in your bliss, and to activate the temple of light that exists within you.

This initiation may be completed as either a self-practice, or as a guided practice whereby the receiver of the initiation is led passively through an internal journey by another. Either way is sufficient; however, in the case of a self-led practice, ensure that the entire process is read and understood before commencement to ensure that the energy created throughout the process is not broken when instructional points are read. You may also choose to record yourself reading the initiation to follow along with later, making sure to allow time to perform each step as instructed.

1. Sit down on a chair or on the ground. Preferably, sit on the earth, the soil, the grass.

2. Close your eyes.

3. Feel your root on Mother Nature. Feel the part of your base that sits on and connects to the earth. Breathe into your base and your connection to Mother Earth beneath you.

4. Feel the pleasure of Mother Earth within your base. As you breathe downwards, activate in your base your pleasure with your intention, your focus, your breath, and a gentle natural movement of your pelvis.

5. Notice the mind as you activate pleasure at your base centre. Does your mind seek to judge this experience? Notice that aspect of your thoughts and dive beyond it, deeper into your pleasure experience, as you connect and activate your base on Mother Earth.

6. Stay in this pleasure-activating movement with deep breathing until you feel your sacred sexual energy spark up and amplify.

7. Now, as you continue to move your pelvis and cultivate pleasure, move your awareness to your heart also and command:

   "I call forth this pleasure into my heart."

8. Can you move and circulate your pelvis, connecting to pleasure at the base while breathing into the heart and its expansive energy?

9. Use the power of your sexual energy at your base to open and activate your heart. Use your movement at the pelvis and your deep orgasmic breath, in through the nose, out of the mouth.

10. Keep building this energy between the base and the heart.

Focus on nothing but your experience of pleasure as you bathe in this energy that you are cultivating.

11. When the energy within your body feels intense, turn your palms up and reach your hands outward and command:

    "I call forth the magic of this ecstasy into my hands."

12. Allow the energy to flow down your arms and into your hands and fingers. Allow your arms to move and flow and dance in whatever way they naturally desire to do.

13. Stay in this free-flowing organic movement of your arms, hands, and pelvis. Maintain a deep and connected breath. Stay connected to the feelings and sensations within the body, and maintain the intention of cultivating more divine pleasure. Observe the mind and move beyond it, deeper into the sensations of the body.

14. This is the activation process. Once you have felt pure bliss and ecstasy in this process, you are ready to command your temple of light activation through this incantation, chanted from your state of bliss-charged ecstasy:

    "Mother/Father God, open me fully to receive your divine grace. Allow me to feel the pleasure of your love as orgasmic bliss in this body vessel. I am with you, and I love you. I dance for you, as you dance through me. Om Tat Sat."

15. You can stay in this bliss-charged state that is your temple of light for as long as you so desire. When you choose to come back or come down, it will always be a choice, because that is the privilege of one who has been initiated into their temple of light.

Remember, this may take practice. To get lost in the full orgasmic pleasure of a simple moment is to transcend the thinking and judging mind fully. To receive this activation, practice getting lost in the feeling, and allow the mind to soften all judgment.

This initiation practice can be carried through into many different activities. Lovemaking, dancing, swimming in the ocean, walking through nature—throughout all of these activities, steps one through thirteen can be followed to initiate pleasure, firstly at the base, then into the heart, and then the hands, in order to circulate pleasure and ecstasy through the entire body while completing the activity.

Remember, you are worthy of this initiation. You are worthy of pleasure. You are worthy of orgasmic ecstasy. Your judgements and shame are loved by God, just as all of you is loved by God. Come with us and let us guide you back to the magic of what it means to be a human being inhabiting your divine earthly human body vessel.

THE SEED OF LIFE

nside the heart of man, there is a seed that can be accessed. It is called "the seed of life." This seed, although small-seeming in nature, has the potential and capacity to grow into boundless love. Boundless love is the true meaning of love—that is, love without limits, love without restrictions, love without obligations, and love without expectations. This quality of boundless love needs to be felt and cultivated in order for you to receive the gift that is the initiation into being a keeper of the light codes.

Boundless love knows no restrictions and therefore cannot be projected at a single person, place, or thing. Boundless love is all-encompassing of light and dark, right and wrong, good and bad. Boundless love does not judge or discriminate; it simply loves all aspects, all elements and intricacies. Without boundless love, you are disconnected from your truth, for the ability to love so limitlessly is what connects us and entwines us with all things. The moment you remember boundless love, you remember the infinite nature of your being, connected and entwined with all of life.

This knowledge of boundless love starts at the heart. It starts as a small seed: the seed of life. This seed sits waiting and pulsing for the sacred moment that it is germinated with the ferocious love of a beating heart. This seed that sits dormant in many wants to be ignited, initiated back to its full potent truth and potential, for it is in this seed that God sits. God is love, and God is always waiting to be remembered.

We are going to show you an initiation that will ask this seed to open. This initiation is the start of the remembering of great love, and this initiation is here to be accessed by you now.

THE INITIATION PRACTICE

This initiation practice is a guided meditation in essence, and for that reason, it is best delivered as such. These written words are best received from a fully surrendered state of being, with eyes closed. This meditation should be read aloud, lovingly and with focus, to the recipient who is ready to receive the Seed of Life Initiation. You may also choose to record yourself reading the initiation to follow along with later, making sure to allow time to perform each step as instructed.

1. Start by lying on the ground on your back. You must lie in this way, for your heart must be facing upwards, and your chest must be open to the sky.

2. Start to breathe in a way that connects you to your heart. Your heart holds the seed of life, so remember this, and feel this knowing as you breathe into your heart centre. This will start to activate the seed immediately.

3. Start to see the seed. See it as a small and simple seed that lies in the void of the chest.

4. Start to breathe into this seed, and feel it as the potential for all of life.

5. As the seed starts to crack open, see a green stem and leaf unravel itself, pointing upwards towards the sun.

6. Allow your breath, your awareness, and your focus to see this now germinated seedling start to grow upwards towards the front of your chest cavity. As the now small tree grows upwards, it becomes stronger and stronger, and so it breaks through the chest wall, bursting upward towards the sky.

7. From the seed of your chest, this great tree continues to grow upwards, up towards the sky. This tree becomes tall and strong as it grows perfectly upward towards the sun and towards the heavens. See this tree and its beautiful leaves blowing gently up into the farthest reach of the blue skies, all the while rooted in your chest, at your heart.

8. As the tree continues its momentum upwards, feel the pull of the roots of your chest. Feel that the tree wants to break free from its roots to continue its journey upwards. And so it does. Feel and see the tree pulling on the roots of your chest until these roots pull away, leaving a deep cavernous void within your chest where the tree and its roots were once embedded.

9. Watch the tree drift up and off into the distance, and now feel what is left in your chest: a black, hollow void from which magnificent life grew. This is the hollow of your heart that knows only life and love.

10. Start to feel the warmth and glow of the sun shining into the hollow of your heart. Let this hollow be bathed in healing, glowing sunlight, and see the walls of the hollow turn to brilliant whitish gold.

11. This is your sacred space of perfection. Here you can feel

all of life, all of love, and all of God. Feel this energy of the hollow of the heart bathed in whitish gold consume you. Allow this energy to consume your whole body. Bathe in this shower of love and life. You are a divine creator. You created life, you are life, you released life, and you repurposed life. You are divine, and you are here now. Om Tat Sat.

THE POWER FLAME

The fourth initiation speaks to the hearts of men—that is, the hearts of men and women that know the ferocious warrior energy. The ferocious warrior energy is that which creates great change on planet Earth. This is the energy that keeps the fire burning for positive change, that keeps the fire burning for continual growth, and that keeps the fire burning for desire and hunger for better. Better is more love, more joy, more righteousness, more courage, more expansiveness, and more truthfulness.

This fire needs to be alive and well in the hearts of all men in order for the Earth to fulfill its destiny as its most realised, most Godly aligned Mother Gaia. Until this point of realisation, all of humanity that isn't connected to their sacred power flame will feel unfulfilled and uninspired.

Within you lives a power flame, a fire of burning desire that burns to serve God and the fulfillment of Mother Earth's most realised glory. This flame seeks to glow and burn so bright that from you springs ferocious action, passion, and divinely inspired creativity. You are meant to feel love, and a desire to lead from that love. You are meant to feel a divinely inspired hunger to leave your mark on the planet, no matter how small or great that mark is. You are meant to feel a selfless surge of energy that pulses you forward into action for the highest good. So, why haven't you felt this energy or flame in the past? Why have you felt stagnant and tired and confused about where to direct your energy? Because you have been tainted, as much of humanity is, by the dull greyish sludge that is the energy of stagnation, bred from separation and isolation from God. It is that simple. Know God, and know where to direct your heart's creative passion flame. Know God, and know with that how to serve God and the planet.

This greyish sludge that is the energy of stagnation is washed over much of humanity at present. Dazed and confused, your human population stares into the void of illusion, wondering and aching for a life that feels vital. Their souls know vitality, but their minds and their bodies cannot fathom how to reach a state of being that they long for and yet cannot completely comprehend. This humanity is separate. Only they exist in their own world, separate from all else. From this space of separation, humanity only can have creativity and passion to serve themselves in one way or another. Service to self will never be fully fulfilling and will never spring from the true passion centre of the heart, and therefore, it will never be supported with the limitless energy, guidance, and power of the Divine.

Do you see? All your work from here on should feel like a ferocious fire of love that cannot be put out. Why? Because God is moving through you. God needs you, and God will use you as a vessel for the divine plan. Open yourself into unity with God, and instantly be ignited with the fire of love and creativity that leaves you with no choice but to spring forth into heart-driven action.

You are here now and ready for this initiation. You are ready to have the passion flame of your heart fully ignited. You know God. You know love. You are open and ready for God to use you as a conduit for the divine plan that is to anchor Heaven on Earth and to uplift the paradigm of suffering back to the Garden of Eden template that it was always intended to be. This is your job as a conduit for spirit, and here, now, you will be ignited.

THE PRACTICE

This initiation is a combination of focused breath, guided meditation, and incantation. This initiation is best received passively and from a receptive state. For this reason, it is best to be guided by a loving and heart-centred partner who can read and lead you through the meditation and breathing while you sit upright in a focused state with the eyes closed. You may also choose to record yourself reading the initiation to follow along with later, making sure to allow time to perform each step as instructed.

The breath described should be followed through the entire meditation, until a state of inward focus is obtained whereby the deepened breath naturally falls away. The incantations are written in bold and need to be read aloud as commands to the subtle energy body. The whole guided meditation should be read aloud, but the incantations should hold a different energy when delivered, as they are prayers rather than meditation instructions.

1. Sit comfortably, preferably cross-legged on the floor, with a tall spine.

2. **"You are ready to bring the fire of God into your heart, to open yourself as a conduit for creativity, passion, and divinely inspired action."**

3. Connect to the heart space. See, sense, and feel the heart space.

4. Start to breathe into the heart, in through the nose and out of the mouth with a sigh. Let the sigh be the authentic

sound of the heart in this moment. Continue with this breath.

5. Really feel the heart and the love and passion that exists here. Use the breath and the sigh to connect to this love and passion.

6. See a tiny flickering ember within the heart.

7. With each breath, give your oxygen to this flame. See the flame growing bigger and brighter. Use your breath to feel the passion and fire of this flame as it burns and grows brighter within your chest.

8. See and feel this fire grow to fill your chest. Use your breath and your sound with each sigh to breathe life and energy into this fire.

9. See, sense, and feel this flame growing taller into your throat and neck. Feel the flame burning through any restriction or limitation at the throat.

10. **"I use this flame to clear away any limitation or restriction at the throat chakra. Open now at the throat fully, as a clear conduit for Divine Spirit."**

11. See, sense, and feel this flame growing taller into your head and your crown.

12. **"I use this flame to clear away any blocks or distortions in my vision and connection to Source. I am open now fully. I see, I sense, and I know."**

13. See, sense, and feel the flame move through the crown of your head and beam from the crown as a white divine light

beam shooting up to the central sun, the centre of the multiverse and all of creation.

14. Sit and feel the flame of your heart that waves and flows from your chest, up your throat, and into your head, and also see the beam of white light that shoots through your crown up to the Infinite. This is the connection of your heart's passion centre to the light divine.

15. **"You are activated now. You are aligned with your soul mission as a conduit for God's love, here to create magic on Earth. Well done. We commend you."**

16. Sit in this divine bath of fire energy, and feel how connected you are, how supported you are, and how loved you are.

17. **"You will soon be called upon for assistance. Listen to our call, and be a selfless servant for Mother Gaia's revival. Let God work through you, and you will always be guided and rewarded. You are activated now. Om Tat Sat."**

THE SHADOW THAT KEPT YOU PRISONER

The shadow that kept you prisoner is the place within you so deep and so unknown that its power and hold cannot be felt until it has been transcended. This place, although dark, is your true ticket into the golden light. This is your route to full liberation: the understanding, acknowledgement, and release of this shadow piece.

To know your shadow is to know yourself fully, for until you can witness and observe every aspect of yourself, you cannot fully meet and know every aspect of God and feel God's infinite love working through you. You cannot know all of God without knowing all of yourself, for you are the Divine in expression—for you are the Divine playing out existence as you!

Knowing the shadow piece is the path to liberation. Many will seek to only know that which is easy to love within themselves. Many will seek to learn the attributes and qualities within that emanate and vibrate as love, joy, and abundance. But as the shadow piece of oneself is bypassed, so too is the ability to meet God in God's full glory. God loves all of you, and until you love all of you too, you will not feel all of God's love. To understand this is to know the path of and to liberation and salvation. Those who dive deep into the shadow body often find the pinnacle of light far sooner than the light seeker. But that is not to say that the shadow body is the only body to explore. To know all of oneself is to know all of God. Therefore, the highest states of ecstasy and transcendence, joy and love must be explored and pursued as well, of course.

This shadow quest—to understand and meet the darkest aspects of the self in order to transmute the dark into light through the power of love, acceptance, and awareness—is the piece of the puzzle that needs to be revisited often. The shadow quest is infinite—that is, infinitely deep, infinitely insightful, and infinitely liberating.

The shadow of self is not a place to wallow or indulge in. It is not a space to fuel the addiction of suffering that plagues humankind. Rather, it is to be seen as a contraction within the energetic body, which once noticed can be felt, acknowledged, loved, and transmuted as a gateway to God. This contraction may be felt as a lower-vibratory emotion, such as sadness, anger, frustration, guilt, shame, or despair. Or this contraction may be felt as energetic density or heaviness.

The shadow work is the work of the brave, the work of the extraordinary ones who know that life itself is nothing short of extraordinary. To dare to dive into the self is to dare to be met fully by all manner of existence. Daring to dive into the unexplored aspects of the self is the quickest path to God, for where there is courage led from the heart, there is always triumph and always an uprising to new states of glory and new states of love.

Journey with us now into your shadow piece—the piece of you that arises now, in this now moment, to be noticed, to be loved, and to be accepted as an aspect of God that is your gateway to purity and truth.

This initiation is best practiced on a day when heavy emotion is present. Such emotion could be frustration, sadness, loneliness, anger, or guilt. It is these emotions that vibrate more densely and allow access to the shadow self. These lower-vibrational emotions are tools, for when emotions such as anger or sadness are felt fully, and with that loved and accepted fully, they are transmuted. Sadness is the gateway to more bliss. Anger is the gateway to more love. When lower-density emotions are ignored, powerful opportunities to experience more light are denied.

For this reason, emotions such as sadness or anger are not "bad." How can something be bad when it is the gateway to more love and God? When lower-vibrational emotions arise within, they are an opportunity for expansion—particularly when these emotions persist.

It is important to understand that heavy emotion that arises from a thought should not be treated as a gateway to God. This emotion can be released and transmuted simply by releasing the thought! The heavy emotion that persists when the mind is clear is what needs to be dived into and felt fully in this initiation practice.

This initiation should be practiced alone. When feeling the emotion that arises, it should never be projected outwards at another person or thing, but rather felt within and expressed through sound, tears, or movement. This initiation practice is about knowing yourself more fully, and nothing that you feel within is ever the fault of another person or experience. Everything that you feel within is an opportunity to understand yourself more fully and is your own responsibility!

THE PRACTICE

1. Sit comfortably. Quiet the mind in whatever way you choose as best you can.

2. Feel your body. Feel how open or closed it feels. What is ready to come up now?

3. Speak these words:

> *"I invite up and I call forth the piece of me that is ready to be felt and loved."*

> *"Where are you, tender place within me that holds my soul prisoner at this time? Show yourself to me now."*

4. As you notice your body, notice the emotion that is present. Do not give the emotion or feeling a name. Do not attach a story to it. Simply notice it, and allow yourself to feel it. Feel it fully as an energy.

5. Notice where the emotion is. Is it in your throat? Is it in your heart? Is it in your gut?

6. Do not shy away from whatever it is that you feel. Stay fully present with the feeling that you notice. Bring all of your awareness to this feeling, and breathe into this feeling.

7. Speak to this feeling:

> *"I will not shy away from you. I am here to give you all of my awareness and presence. I accept you fully."*

8. Keep breathing into this feeling, allowing it to intensify.

9. Allow this emotion to become itself fully, and from that, feel and express whatever that is fully—rage, disgust, sadness, fear, shame. Allow tears to flow, allow anger to be expressed, allow anything that feels natural and authentic.

10. Now stay with this practice for as long as possible. Make sure there is no story attached to the emotion and no thoughts

of the mind perpetuating the process. This is a process of feeling and expressing only.

11. When it feels as though there is nothing left to feel, sit and notice the body again. Notice if the feeling, the energy has moved. If it has, then begin the process again and continually until you feel neutral.

12. From this neutral space, can you find love? This emotion that sat dormant within you, waiting to be noticed and waiting to be loved, has now been noticed. Can you find love for the emotion that you just experienced?

13. Breathe into love.
    Breathe into love for your ability to feel.
    Breathe into love for your ability to be vulnerable.
    Breathe into love for your courage to express yourself authentically.
    Breathe into love for the acceptance you have for yourself.

14. "I open now to experience more love. I allow light to flood into my body and energy system. I am the Light Divine."

Om Tat Sat; and so it is.

Once the keeper of the light codes within is fully initiated, the shadow self is continually recognised, acknowledged, and transmuted with little effort, for where there is true unconditional love, all is accepted and transmuted in an instant. Return to this practice often and when needed, and over time, it will become less needed along your journey towards liberation.

THE AWAKENING OF THE GURU WITHIN

This initiation speaks to the aspect of you that seeks to be initiated. This is the step in the process where you learn—or rather, remember—that there was never an initiation that was needed in the first place! You were born perfect. You were born a spark of the Infinite. You were born a sacred expression of God. And therefore, there has never truly been anything for you to be initiated into, but rather drawn back to, unraveled into, and broken down into.

Your true essence is God. You were born as that, and only over time and years of experiences have you come to forget that on some level. When you were a baby, there was never anything for you to become, learn, or strive for. You were it! You were perfect as God's creation. And then over the years, more and more was expected of you, by yourself or by those around you. And from that expectation, you forgot your perfection. You forgot that you were God incarnated and that there was nothing for you to become.

So, as God incarnated, who must initiate you? YOU. Who must induct you into your holiest rite of passage? YOU. Who is your master, your guru that gives you permission to walk the ascended righteous path? YOU. You are all of these things and always have been, since birth and far beyond. Since the seed of your soul was born out of the flicker of light that is the divine central sun, you always were and always will be a perfect expression of God, whether that is realised fully or waiting to be remembered.

Now you must realise that these words do not initiate you. Now you must realise that these practices do not initiate you. YOU initiate you into your place as a keeper of the light codes. Your soul essence that has always been God seeps into the aspects of you that have forgotten their perfection in this moment. You rescue you. You uplevel you. You remember the God that you are. Why? Because no one else can. All the while someone or something else is the master, the guru, the initiator, you have forgotten the God that you are.

These words, this book, these practices, they are here to wake up the dormant guru within. These words hold no power without your infinite power to receive them. You are the conduit and the transmitter for the light of these words, and therefore, these words hold no light without you. Can you see now the power that you are? This book is here to serve you, the guru waiting to remember. This book is here to serve you as a reminder of the power that you already are and always have been. You do not need to change. You do not need to upgrade. How could a manifestation of God's perfection ever need to change? You simply need to remember that you are a manifestation of divine perfection, and come back to that remembering in every moment.

So, who may take the role of your teacher in this lifetime? Only those individuals who serve to remind you of the master that you are. Only those teachers who wish to reach into your heart and clutch at the magic that you hold there, simply to help you remember that magic. You do not ever need to look up to another with anything other than love, for to worship another as having more wisdom, more greatness, or more potential is to forget the perfection of God's most perfect creation: you. You are it, and your world simply mirrors your perfection back to you.

Let go now of the need to ever be saved, taught, inducted, or initiated. You needn't look any further than into your own soul wisdom for the greatest truths and teachings that have ever been told. And as you take this practice of the sixth initiation, do so as your greatest teacher, as your greatest healer, and feel the magic that you are. The true guru is the guru within. Ong namo guru dev namo, I bow to the divine teacher within.

THE PRACTICE

This practice is very simple, but infinitely powerful. Use an alarm to time eleven minutes to ensure that you are not distracted by watching the clock. Stay in closed-eyed, focused meditation for the entire eleven minutes, and remain in meditation for as long as needed after the process is finished. You may also choose to record yourself reading the initiation to follow along with later, making sure to allow time to perform each step as instructed.

1. Sit with the eyes closed, cross-legged if possible, with the spine tall.

2. Rest the hands on the knees with the palms turned up.

3. Centre yourself by breathing into the body and coming away from the mind.

4. For eleven minutes, repeat the following two steps over and over again.

5. In the mind, say, *"With this sound, I wake up and remember the guru within."*

6. Out loud, chant the sound OM: "Aaauuuuummmm."

7. Repeat.

8. As you chant the sound OM, allow yourself to feel the vibration of your sound as it wakes up the aspect of God that lives within every cell and every fibre of your being.

This is your awakening and remembering back to God consciousness—the God that you already are. Om Tat Sat.

YOUR BODY IS A GATEWAY INTO THE ETERNAL COSMOS

The seventh initiation is not one to shy away from. This is your reckoning. This is your moment of magic amidst the chaos of life. This initiation is to spellbind you into something far more mystical and sacred than your mind can comprehend. Your body can feel and remember how magic you are. Your body holds the openings, the portals, the gateways, the caves back to nirvana, and because of that, your body knows what it is to be magic. But your mind has forgotten and hasn't wished to remember—but now, remember it shall.

You are a portal back to the mystical kingdom of transcendent love and liberation. You yourself, your own body is a gateway into the eternal cosmos of mysticism and magic. You can stop now and try to understand this, or you can continue on to truly know and feel this.

We are going to show you how limitless you are. You are bound by nothing. Once you remember the portal that you are, you are no longer fixed to a single reality, a single time, or a single place. Once you access the aspect of yourself that is your own doorway to infinity, you become infinity, and you dissolve any aspect of you that is not infinite. We are going to help you now to open up to that. We are going to help you to remember that your body is a gateway to your true expansive nature. We want you to feel this now.

THE PRACTICE

This initiation practice is a guided meditation. This initiation practice is best received passively and from a receptive state. For this reason, it is best to be guided by a loving and heart-centred partner who can read and lead you through the meditation while you sit upright or lie comfortably in a focused state with the eyes closed. You may also choose to record yourself reading the initiation to follow along with later, making sure to allow time to perform each step as instructed.

1. Lie down or sit tall, and close your eyes.

2. Cast your imagination to the stars, the galaxies, the cosmos.

3. Feel yourself floating in the expansive blackness of the cosmos, and be here fully.

4. Feel your body dissolve into the blackness of the cosmos. Who is now floating? Simply your awareness; your consciousness is floating in space.

5. Can you feel the seed that is your consciousness dissolve into the blackness of the cosmos? Who is left? Simply the infinite cosmos, and you are a part of it. You *are* it.

6. Now stay here, fully immersed with all of the cosmos, fully remembered as the oneness that you are.

7. Where do you wish to go? Where do you want to explore?

What do you want to see? Invite yourself on a journey through the cosmos, and know that nothing is off limits.

8. Take yourself to the space that will show you exactly what you need to see in this moment. What is there? Where are you?

9. You are free to explore now. You have been freed from any limitations and are now the infinite cosmic explorer of all of time and space. Enjoy this journey, and remember that you are only ever journeying through yourself, for you are it. Om Tat Sat.

THE TURN OF THE BLUE KEY

The turn of the blue key is the start of the entrance into nirvana. Nirvana is where magnificence starts and paradise is felt on all levels. Where is nirvana, and how is it entered? It starts with the turn of the blue key. This phrase is coded, for the blue key is a metaphor, an energetic representation of that which grants you access to paradise. So, what is the blue key literally? It is everything that allows you to feel God consciousness. The blue key is everything that opens you to absolute connection with the Divine and the infinite nature of the present moment as experienced by you. When we speak of the blue key, we speak of all that gets you there, all that aligns you to that vibration.

Why blue? Blue is the colour of alignment. Blue pulls you into focus, into poignancy, into truth. Blue is the colour that is the portal to infinity, and therefore, a blue key means more than you know.

The blue key is coming now, into your field, to be held tightly in your hand. Use it to attain access to the golden life, to the nirvana that awaits you in all moments. The blue key has to be activated to be effective in unlocking the paradise realm. Are you ready to have access to the fully activated blue key? Are you ready to receive the gift of that which opens the portal to paradise? You are ready for this initiation. Do not overthink it. Once the blue key has been handed to you, it is there, it is imprinted in the palm of your hand to never leave you.

THE PRACTICE

This practice is very simple. Read the instructions first, then guide yourself through this short journey. Close your eyes for this journey, but open them briefly to read out the incantation.

1. Sit and bring all of your awareness to the palm of your right hand. Keep your focus there fully.

2. Read aloud, *"I am ready to activate and imprint the blue key of truth and life without limits into my hand now to set me free. OM TAT SAT."*

3. See, sense, and feel a blue key appear in the palm of your right hand.

4. Use the middle finger of your left hand to press the key into the right palm.

5. Feel how the key begins to merge with your skin and with your body.

6. The key becomes invisible. It is fully activated now, and thus it is merged with your energetic field.

7. Sit in this knowing and in the feeling that comes from this knowing for a few minutes.

You are now the portal to nirvana. Trust that there is nothing left to do or understand for this initiation, but know that you are opening more and more each day to higher levels of bliss. The paradise matrix is being constructed for you in your physical world. You have the key now to be held in permanency in the paradise matrix. Feel these words as the conclusion of this initiation and know that you are being set free.

And so it is.

THE PARADIGM OF LOVE AND POWER

We give you this gift now to help you to see and understand the paradigm of love and power that is present in all things. Love and power are not opposing; neither are they similar. They are two energies that run parallel to each other, one vibrating at a higher resonance and one at a slightly lower resonance. Love and power are two harmonies of the same symphony, and therefore, the beauty and power of the symphony cannot be felt in its entirety without both harmonies present.

To understand this better and why this is important to your life, let us cast your vision back to a day where you felt turmoil. Perhaps the world was weighing heavy on your shoulders? Perhaps you felt lost and confused by the infinite potential of the future beyond your control? Whatever the reason for the turmoil, cast your vision back to that day. Who were you on that day? You were but a mere mortal. You were someone who was so very tired. An energy of death loomed. And why did you need to feel that on that particular day? To remind you of the love that you are and to remind you of the power that you are.

Without love, you are powerless, and yet without power, you can be full of love. So, on that day of turmoil where you held no power, only powerlessness, could you find love? Could you find love and kindness for yourself in your moment of despair? Could you find love for the simplicity of life on that day in the beauty of a bird in a tree or a stranger at the park? And could you find love for that day of turmoil? Were you able to see that day as a blessing full of love that allowed you to retreat to the sacred internal space of the heart, your eternal refuge from suffering? And perhaps if you could do this, if you could find love on that day of turmoil, could you then reignite your power? Could you feel that in your nothingness and despair, you were more powerful than ever?

If you can love yourself in nothingness and despair, then you become infinitely powerful, for you then hold the gift that is the power to feel love in absolutely every moment. And isn't this surely the ticket that sets you free of suffering eternally? So, love and power are not separate, but nor are they the same. You hold more power than you can imagine when you tap into love of that which is deemed unlovable.

To love a stray dog so fully that the dog is reborn into its full courage, strength, and radiance—that is to harness the power of love.

To love the intensity of the pain of labor so fully that the pain transforms into an activation of the sun, the stars, the cosmos, and the womb, all within the physical body—that is to harness the power of love.

To love an illness within you so deeply that the illness no longer limits you, but liberates you, because you become so fearless and so at peace—that is to harness the power of love.

To love the idea of death, of self or another, so fully that the idea of life is transformed completely into one that is boundless, limitless, and carefree—that is to harness the power of love.

So, what is it that we are trying to explain?

Let these simple words be your practice…

We want you to find more love in your most challenging times. We want you to feel your pain, feel your despair, your hardship, your suffering as it arises—and then we want you to love it. Love it as a child that needs to be loved. Love yourself as a child that needs to be loved. Love whatever you experience on your day of turmoil so deeply that the matrix of suffering shatters, and you are set free—set free into the ultimate power, which is the freedom to feel only love even on the darkest of days. For when you can find love on the darkest day, your heart illuminates the path to your salvation, and from there, you can never look back.

THE JOURNEY BACK TO FREEDOM AND SOVEREIGNTY

This is a big initiation, a big piece of the puzzle, and thus it holds the position of number ten, the holy number, for this is the holiest of initiations.

This is where we want you to take stock of what you have learned and integrated thus far. Who are you on your journey to being a keeper of the light codes? You are you, infinitely perfect and infinitely divine. You have made it this far to receive these words in the following chapters, and therefore, you are more ready to claim your mastery than you know.

Your mastery comes in the form of this moment now, whereby you remember the God/Goddess that you are. Bound by nothing, bound by no one. Bound by no fixed idea, contract, or bond. Bound by no shackle of old wounding or old identities. You are limitless, and you are here now, reading these words and remembering this truth. We love you, and we commend you for coming this far. This initiation, that which we have labelled "number ten," is the start of something different for you: a new way of thinking, feeling, and believing, a new way of gliding through life on the wings of God's grace, held up by the sea of infinity that is God's creation. You are reading this now for you to know your perfection and to know that all is done. No further work is needed.

You have arrived at the holiest of holies that is your life at this current conjuncture point, in front of what is old and behind what is new and unfolding, suspended in the present moment, waiting for what is to arrive next. Here it is; this is what is to arrive next...

What is to arrive next is your liberation, your true freedom and sovereignty, for when you remember that which we have just told you, you have no limits. You are God. You are God's grace, and therefore, you begin to engage with life as that, answering to no one, bound by no rule or no enslavement. Rise up, dear one, and claim your throne as the true sovereign of your body, your land, your universe, your eternity. You are it, and that is that. Om Tat Sat. And so it is.

And now we sit with you as you embark on a meditation, a feat that is truly for you to remember your power as a free and sovereign divine one, fully realised and activated. Claim your throne now.

THE PRACTICE

Read the practice thoroughly to truly understand the instructions, then guide yourself through this simple meditation and breath exercise while sitting. Alternatively, receive this practice passively and from a receptive state as guided by a loving and heart-centred partner who can read and lead you through the meditation and breath while you sit upright. You may also choose to record yourself reading the initiation to follow along with later, making sure to allow time to perform each step as instructed.

1. Sit on the seat that holds your full power as the divine sovereign king/queen that you are.

2. See this seat and the majesty that it holds. It is not of this 3D realm, and neither are you. So, sit on this magical throne, and as you do so, claim it as your own.

3. Drink from the golden chalice the elixir that is your remembering and your initiation of your divine power.

4. Breathe in the air that surrounds you, and feel it as God's grace massaging your lungs, your insides, your cells.

5. Hold a golden crown in your hands and gaze upon it. Place the golden majestic crown of your initiation upon your head. Feel the weightlessness of this divine crown as it rests upon your head. It belongs on your head, divine one. You are the sovereign ruler of your kingdom, powerful and ignited for eternity. Om Tat Sat.

THE ELEVENTH CHAKRA: THE GATEWAY TO COSMIC CONSCIOUSNESS

The Soul Star chakra, or the eleventh chakra, is located as a halo above your head. See it as a vortex or a spinning halo that aligns you and connects you to cosmic consciousness. This chakra lies on a straight point upward vertically, connecting you to the heavens and the infinite worlds above you. This chakra point, the spinning halo or vortex, lies six feet above your head at a point in space that is the outermost limit of your own auric field. It sits at the upper edge of the limit of your own personal cosmic identity.

Why is the eleventh chakra important for you to understand now? It has long been forgotten. The crown or seventh chakra has been viewed and understood as the cosmic portal to the infinite; however, this is not entirely the case. The crown chakra grants access to the Akasha and to your memory of infinite soul lifetimes, but it is not infinitely *cosmic* in nature and energy. The crown connects you beyond this lifetime and beyond that which you can see and perceive to your greatest understanding of life through your higher mind. However, the Soul Star chakra is responsible for your connection to all realms beyond time and space. The Soul Star chakra is your gateway to God, other solar systems, other realms, and other dimensions and galaxies. This is the chakra that, once activated and aligned, is your passport and portal to the infinity of space and beyond. When this chakra has been activated, the human in question becomes superhuman in nature—that is, not bound by the limitations of their perceived physical reality or location.

Would you like to travel anywhere in space in an instant through the cosmic internal passageway that is the Soul Star chakra? Would you like to journey beyond your body, your home, and your planet to experience infinity and all that could potentially exist within it? Well, it is time to let go of the notion that that is not possible and open to the truth that is your galactic nature. Your physical body is your anchor to your planet Earth. Where one can transcend their physical body, one can transcend their planet Earth through inward travel and teleportation of consciousness.

Your universe and beyond is intended to be explored by the Creator. How are you to explore it? Through the portal within your own auric field, the Soul Star chakra, the spinning halo six feet above your head. This is your passport and portal to space and other realms.

This portal has been forgotten and shut down for much of your known history. Attacks have taken place on this floating chakra centre in an attempt to confuse the ideologies of humanity. When humanity is disconnected from their cosmic consciousness, humanity will fail to understand their true gifts, powers, talents, and cosmic nature. A humanity disconnected from cosmic consciousness will only know and understand their physical body as an anchor point to planet Earth, and all else beyond that will hold no value or merit. When humanity knows the true nature of its cosmic consciousness, then the understanding of the physical body and how it relates to planet Earth shifts entirely. Less focus is given to the physical body, for it is but one body and one small aspect of the true nature of self. To know this is to know God.

Humanity must now start to awaken to the true nature of its cosmic consciousness. Via an activated eleventh Soul Star chakra, you must start to remember the galactic beacon of light that you are, ready to transcend your physical body at any time to venture far beyond time and space into the infinity of all other worlds. You can do this. You are a human being, and therefore, this is your gift, given to you by God, always waiting to be seen and acknowledged.

How can we now explain this differently? We want you to hold a deep understanding of this topic. When you close your eyes, your world disappears. The world that seems so real to you fades instantly simply by you closing your eyes. And when you close down your thoughts, all of your internal attachments to that world disappear instantly, for it was only the thoughts making them so. And when you still your body completely, the body disappears instantly, for it was only your interaction with the physical body that was making it real. So, what is left with no vision of the external world, no thought, and no movement? Consciousness—pure consciousness.

The mind that can observe the experience of no thought: that is your pure consciousness. And then, from this space of silent witness, a world above you is seen and perceived. A cosmic space of no limits exists, and you can feel it, although perhaps you cannot see it or fully understand it. But then, when you cast your awareness to the spinning halo six feet above your head, you feel that the bridge between worlds begins to dissolve. The bridge between you and the cosmic heavens begins to dissolve, and your awareness lands in the cosmic heavens. You can be here now for an infinite amount of time; you can be here now for all of eternity, for the notion of time does not exist here. This is where you are from, and where you shall return, from and to the galactic mind of the Creator that holds all of creation. You can explore, you can connect, you can cast your energy out or anchor higher energies in. You are the alchemist in this space, and you are free.

And when you choose to come back—back into your physical body, back into your anchor to the Earth realm—you will feel lighter in your body, for it will hold less weight, it will hold less meaning. You are not this body, no. You are the eternal cosmic consciousness, experiencing life on Earth in a physical body, and you can dance between these two knowings, taking neither more seriously than the other.

THE PRACTICE

We take you on this journey now to ask you to remember and activate your Soul Star chakra.

This needs to be done slowly, for to rush this activation is to potentially miss the full upgrade of frequency that can and will take place.

1. Give yourself time to rest in a position that allows you to deeply surrender, out of the body and out of the mind.

2. Relax deeply, close to the threshold of sleep, but without crossing that threshold. Take yourself between worlds with your own deep relaxation.

3. Set the intention to activate fully your Soul Star chakra.

4. See the spinning halo six feet above your head, and stay with this for as long as your awareness will allow.

5. Allow the speed of the spinning halo and vibrancy of its glow to intensify as time goes on.

6. You will know when the Soul Star chakra has been fully

activated. The knowing will be deep, and you must trust it. Do not question it. You have done enough, and this galactic portal has been opened.

Welcome to the start of your galactic exploration. Om Tat Sat.

THE KEEPERS OF DIVINE CHANCE AND GRACE

This initiation is to cast you into the light of the unknown. The unknown in itself is a divine gateway to God. In the unknown, there can only be surrender, nonattachment, liberation, and freedom. We invite you now through this initiation to remember the unknown and the power that it holds. The unknown is the future of all human beings. The unknown is not certain, and it is not fixed. The unknown is where you are heading. You cannot plan for it, you cannot dream of it, you cannot will it, and yet it is coming; be sure of that. To plan for the unknown is to plan for nothing. To give energy to the unknown is to waste such energy. And yet the future—your future—is simply that: unknown. To sit in the understanding that the future is unknown and be fully at peace with that understanding is to cast yourself into an energy of absolute freedom and liberation.

For many on your planet, the future is a source of much concern because of its unknown nature. To soften or control that concern, human beings practice many different coping mechanisms. Witchery and sorcery attempt to see and grasp the details of the future in an attempt to make it more "known." Obsessive goal setting and over-planning are an attempt to control the details of the future and pull them into alignment with a vision. Manifestation and dreaming of a future that would be most ideal are an attempt to allow that vision to take hold in one's current reality, as though the unknown future is somehow known and happening now. All of these practices are real and valid. All of these practices are gifts to humanity to help with the difficulty that is full mastery and acceptance of the unknown nature of the future. But when one can fully understand that absolutely nothing is fixed or guaranteed, and in that understanding, expand into excitement, love, and trust, then one is liberated of all feelings of sorrow or attachment to the future.

You see, the future is a gift to you from God. Work hard now to open, expand, and connect to Source love, and your future will be the reward you have been waiting for. Your future is your infinite reminder of the love that you are. Commit yourself to God and the selfless path, and all is promised to you—all wisdom, all love, all abundance, all ease, all grace, and all glory. If your commitment to your present moment is always the anchor of your focus, then your future will be more than anything that you can visualise, conceptualise, plan for, or manifest. Instead, it will be divine in nature, an absolute construction of God's vision and God's grace. Your future will be all of this and more if you stop trying so hard to shape it and make it. Let it be. Let it move to you. You do not need to do anything to move to it. Your future is coming. It is guaranteed.

Your mastery comes in this now moment, where you ask yourself, "How can I best serve now? How can I best rise into my mastery and anchor in God consciousness now? And from this, what do I need to do now to serve my future self?" These questions ensure that you are on your path to glory. These questions ensure that your future is divinely paved.

When you cast your vision into the future and look at who you wish to be, and obsess over this fictional character, as though he/she is something that must be pursued, your actions in the present moment become tainted. You begin to make decisions based on the pursuit of an ideal, constructed from your egoic mind. Instead, allow yourself to be with yourself fully now, fully today. Connect to the most divinely inspired aspect of you today. What does he/she want to do? How does he/she want to serve? And if you continued every day to connect to that higher energy, where would that energy day by day guide you as it flowed you into your future? It would connect you to God more and more. And in that, life will become more gracious and more extraordinary day by day as it becomes more infused with the love of the Divine.

So you see, to give up on your dreams of the future isn't to give up on yourself; quite the opposite. Yourself, you, only exist NOW. To give up on your dreams for the future is to invest yourself fully into YOU in this present moment, the only you that will ever exist! And in doing so, you are guaranteeing yourself the most divine future, absolutely unknown and absolutely dancing with the glory of God.

This is something we have to teach humanity urgently. Humanity has lost its way through overplanning and over-conceptualising its future. A one-, five-, ten-, and twenty-year plan is shaped by the limitations of a thinking conscious mind. The reality of what one, five, ten, or twenty years could bring is truly limitless! And so, release the planning. Release the goal setting. Release the idealisation and the manifestation. All hold the notions of escapism from the present moment and attachment to an outcome, neither of which are serving the human energy system. Let go and dive into the present moment, and all of the joy and love that is there to be felt. This is your gateway to your true creativity, your true passionate fire and spark for service. It is from this energy, found here in this present moment, that you create a future so far beyond anything that your mind can comprehend now.

So many would ask now, "What about those people who have no goals, no hopes, no dreams, and yet week by week dwell in a slumber of sadness, are not of service, and are not creating a divinely inspired life?" Well, ask yourself about those people, are they committing to their present moment fully? Or are they lost in another fictional reality, such as those presented by the television or a smartphone? Are they committing to service to others? Or are they addicted to serving themselves and serving their own suffering? Is their intention to expand and connect to God? Or is their intention to chase instant gratification and hedonistic pleasure? This is what we want you to understand. To release your dreams because you have no zest for life is not the same as releasing your dreams because you love life so fully— that is, life in its only form, life in the present moment.

You are that! You are the lover of life who is taking part in this holy initiation. You are the one who is rising up to the greatest heights of love and divinity. You are the one committed to the inward quest of remembering and coming home to purity. And therefore, you are the one who is wise enough and holy enough to release all dreams and attachment to the future, in order to carve out and shape a future spectacular beyond comprehension through the incredible vibrational upgrade that occurs through commitment to service and truth in the present moment. Dare to do this. Dare to dive deep into the present moment and life itself. Dare to release all goals and attachment to outcomes. Dare to trust that the life that is being carved out for you by the Divine *is* divine. You are a keeper of the light codes, and therefore, your future is paved in gold. Trust that this fact is certain, and know that you are ready to receive more magic than you can ever comprehend. All of this magic and more lies in the wild and unknown space of the future—your future.

THE PRACTICE

For now, we want to share with you this practice. This practice is designed to take you deeper into trust of the future and the unknown. This practice is designed to blast away doubt and fear that can lead to an obsessive and controlling relationship with the future.

This initiation practice is a guided meditation. This initiation practice is best received passively and from a receptive state. For this reason, it is best to be guided by a loving and heart-centred partner who can read and lead you through the meditation while you lie comfortably in a focused state with the eyes closed. You may also choose to record yourself reading the initiation to follow along with later, making sure to allow time to perform each step as instructed.

1. Lie out flat on your back.

2. Let go of all thought and all attachment to the world around you. Be here now fully.

3. Can you relax the body to such a degree that you can focus on the heartbeat? Keep going inward and sharpening your focus until you can connect with the ever-so-subtle beat of the heart. Feel and stay connected to it. This beat of your heart is the beat of the cosmic drum. All of the cosmos, all of infinity has a beat, one pulse, one rhythm, one mind: the cosmic mind.

4. Can you stay with the beat of your heart and feel that you are but an aspect of the cosmic web of life, beating in harmony and in unison? Take time to be with this notion. Be with the cosmic drum of your heart. Be with the beat of all of life. Be with the beat of all of infinity. Your heart is one beat of the cosmic symphony, playing perfectly in time.

5. This beat of your heart, it gives you life, it connects you to all things, it is your galactic gateway to all things. And what do you need to do to ensure its perfection? Absolutely nothing. All that you can ever do is observe and love its perfection.

6. Allow yourself to observe and be led by the wave of magic

that is infinitely flowing through you and around you. You are ready now to let go. Let go fully, and let the divine energy of universal perfection guide you always and lovingly forward in absolute flow and harmony with the cosmic drum.

7. Listen to and then repeat these mantras:

> *"I flow and move with the beat of the cosmic drum."*

> *"I give myself to trust and service, and I receive always guidance and grace."*

> *"I bow to the unknown, I choose the unknown, for in the unknown lies God's grace."*

> *"I am ready to accept the mystery and magic of life fully and all that that entails."*

> *"Om Tat Sat."*

STEP INTO MASTERY

This initiation is designed to take you deep into your mastery, to that space within that holds all answers and all knowing. We want you to take this initiation seriously, for once it is completed, you are a master—that is, a master of your pain, a master of your healing, a master of your light body, and a master of your ascension. We know that this is possible for you, so do not question or judge this initiation. You are here, reading this book, reading this chapter, and resonating with these messages, and so, you are already in your mastery, although perhaps it is unrealised. So, this initiation is not magic and powerful; rather, *you* are magic and powerful, and this initiation is merely a tool for your realisation. We want you to know now that you are ready to hold yourself in a way that you never have before. You are ready to guide yourself through your greatest transformation and the greatest leg of your journey to light.

Mastery comes when you let go of the need for anything to be one way or another. Mastery comes when you allow and accept everything and witness without judgment all that exists internally and externally, for turmoil, despair, and frustration only arise from a lack of acceptance of an internal state of being or an external situation. From acceptance, we begin to move into mastery. If you cannot only accept but love everything as it arises, then you move into a state of flow and true nonresistance. When you can allow yourself to flow and move with the world around you and within you, you are always guided infinitely upward towards your true and fully realised ascended glory. So, mastery is not to be perfect. Mastery is not to always be in bliss or always be in joy. Mastery is not to always be absolutely ecstatic with an external scenario. Mastery is to allow and witness all without judgment and with acceptance and love.

Internally, pain will arise. You will experience dark days, just as you experience light. You will experience internal states of being that are less easy to love and accept. Can you love and accept them anyway? Can you accept fully that which you previously may have deemed unacceptable? Can you accept everything about yourself that exists in this present moment? What are you thinking now? What are you feeling now? Who do you perceive yourself to be now? Can you accept and love all of it now? This is your mastery, for when you truly accept and love infinitely all that you are in any given moment, resistance ends, flow begins, and you are met with the grace of God.

Externally, pain will arise. A person that you may feel is intolerable may enter your space. A situation that may feel difficult or even shattering may arise. You may be pushed to a breaking point by a situation that feels so far beyond your control. Is there a situation, person, or thing in this present moment that is challenging you? Can you choose to accept that situation or person exactly as it is now? Can you accept it/them in their entirety? Can you even allow yourself to love that person or situation, knowing that they are or it is giving you the perfect lesson in this now moment to initiate you into your mastery?

Mastery comes when you see all of it, internally and externally, as a blessing—perhaps not an easy blessing to receive, but a blessing nonetheless. Mastery comes when you can laugh at your rage and sweetly smile at your sadness. Mastery comes when you can see the perpetrator who made you a victim as an imperfect child of God who is worthy of your forgiveness.

You hold the keys to mastery now. Your mastery starts now. We want you to let go of any idea that you are not a master, or that you are not ready. You are. And so, now you can begin to change the way that you approach yourself, others, and all situations: as a blessing, always. Mastery takes practice, but it is this simple understanding that can be implemented and practiced by you, always, from here going forward. Find the blessing always, love the blessing always, and with that, transmute all suffering into love and step into true mastery.

Om Tat Sat.

THE POWER
TO CREATE

The fourteenth initiation is one of utmost importance. This initiation speaks to your bravery and courage—that is, your sacred ability to face the day with full fire, full focus, full willingness, and yet a sense of grace and flow. This initiation wants to align you with that part of you that is fearless, that cares not about any ideas of failure or disappointment. This initiation wants to align you with strength, courage, and ambition.

To be aligned with God and have God's grace flowing through you on any given day means that you will be challenged to live your most extraordinary life. Your most extraordinary life will not always be easy. Your most extraordinary life will require you to step up and step out. Your most extraordinary life will require you to reveal your talents to the world and to work hard in ensuring that none of your gifts are left hidden or unrealised. To step up into your full potential and step out into the world requires courage, bravery, and fearlessness.

A life aligned with God requires you to be a selfless servant of God's divine plan. God will use you in the way that only you can be used. God will use you in a way that showcases and highlights all of your unique gifts, talents, and power. God will show you the path, and then you must rise up in action and service. God will show you the path, and then you must do the work. You cannot shy away from your sacred mission. You must be fearless, and you must fulfill your role, regardless of your comfort zone. In fact, your divine mission will make you uncomfortable at times. Your divine mission will challenge you, because it will upgrade you and evolve you into your most fully realised self.

Power, love, excitement, glory: this is the life of one who is fully aligned with their divine mission and living out that mission day by day, despite all challenges and fears.

You are being asked now to listen. Listen to your heart that tells you how to be of service. Perhaps you don't know how that will look in the future, but how does it look today? Today is the only day that exists. Where is your sacred energy being pulled today? Listen, and then do. Move beyond fear, move beyond doubt, and step up today. Step up today, and listen to your heart. Your divine mission in all of its entirety doesn't need to be known by you today. All that needs to be known and felt is the longing of your heart to guide your energy today. Write today. Sing today. Share today. Create today. What will your creation today turn into tomorrow? Perhaps you know; perhaps you don't. Regardless, if you step up today and follow the passion flame of your heart, tomorrow you will be guided to create in a way that leads you further down the sacred path of your divine mission.

What could stop you from stepping up and stepping out today? Perhaps fear, perhaps procrastination, perhaps doubt, perhaps unworthiness. Move beyond all of these. You are a servant of God, and your creation today is not about you, it is about humanity and the realisation of Heaven on Earth. So do it. Do it without judgment. Do it without wondering where it will lead. Do it without wondering if you are doing it well. Create from your heart today with passion, fire, and discipline, and be rewarded tomorrow with clarity of vision and a deeper understanding of your mission here on planet Earth.

Your bravery is needed now. Go and create, go and share your gifts, and be a fearless warrior for the New Earth.

THE PORTAL AT THE BACK OF YOUR HEART

The fifteenth initiation is going to take you somewhere that you have not been before: the portal at the back of your heart that can open you to eternal truth. You need to know now that this portal sits dormant within all beings until activated and opened. Once activated and opened, this portal will allow you to access and remember truth at the deepest level.

This portal has been known and understood by many ancient and wise ones on your planet, but today it is to be known and understood by you. This portal leads to all knowing and truth without question. To access this portal is to access the deepest layer of the fabric of your being.

Are you ready to be opened and activated at the portal at the back of your heart now?

THE PRACTICE

This initiation practice is a guided meditation. This initiation practice is best received passively and from a receptive state. For this reason, it is best to be guided by a loving and heart-centred partner who can read and lead you through the meditation while you lie comfortably in a focused state with the eyes closed. You may also choose to record yourself reading the initiation to follow along with later, making sure to allow time to perform each step as instructed.

1. Close your eyes.

2. Guide yourself to the back of your heart, the space at the back of your spine between your shoulder blades. Allow your awareness to settle here with your breath.

3. See a very tiny circle here, an opening.

4. With your awareness and focus, watch this circular opening at the back of your spine grow and expand until it is the size of your entire mid-back.

5. Stay here with your awareness, and feel the energy of this opened portal.

6. Know that you are activated and opened here now.

7. Receive this incantation...

> *"I call forth the beings of light to reach me through this open portal of communication. I allow myself to receive the wisdom and guidance of the holy ones. I cast the boundaries of this open portal at absolute purity, truth, and wisdom. Om Tat Sat. And with that, I am opened."*

FREEDOM FROM THE CLOCK

The sixteenth initiation is a simple teaching and understanding. It relates to time and how you use it and move through it. When you look at the time on a clock or a watch, what does it tell you? It tells you that there is a single trajectory, a single linear flow of all events that leads infinitely forward to a point in time too far forward to imagine. As the second hand on the clock ticks, it tells you that you are running out of time, that time is passing by and there is nothing that you can do about it. There is a helplessness attached to the ticking clock, for there is nothing that you can do about its ticking.

But what if time as you know it had no meaning and no true importance? You would be free rather than a slave to the clock. Time wants to keep you prisoner. The clock wants to keep you to a deadline and a schedule. What if there were no clocks and no means for measuring time in this way? All deadlines would dissolve, and you would be free. You would be free to move through life based on the natural flow and rhythm of you. Your movements wouldn't be dictated by the clock, but rather by your heart and your desires.

If all the clocks disappeared now, you would create today from your heart's burning desire, and continue to create until such a moment where you felt content and complete. If the clocks disappeared now, you would make love with your beloved and lie in each other's arms until a moment where your union felt truly complete. If the clocks disappeared now, nothing would stop you from walking into the forest and venturing deeper than you have ever ventured, with no worry about when you would make your way back.

The truth is, the clocks do not need to disappear, but rather your attachment and devotion to them do. What aspects of your life are keeping you prisoner to the clock? Living life in service to God, aligned with your divine mission, always allows for full liberation from linear time slavery. Living a life where you and your family are connected to the Earth, real food, and real community as well always allows for full liberation from linear time slavery. You have the ability to free yourself from the need to be devoted to the ticking clock. When you allow this devotion to dissolve, you reattune to the infinite ways that nature attempts to keep you flowing with divine timing.

The rising and setting sun allows you to attune to the hours of work, rest, and play. The grumbling tummy and the desires of your appetite allow you to attune to food and your nutrition needs. The dips and surges of your energy allow you to know when to create with fire and when to soften and recharge.

The clock has allowed your humanity to lose its connection to all of its most pure, natural, and perfect rhythms. The sun rising and setting, the tides of the ocean, the hibernation of a butterfly, the gestation of a baby—none of these use a clock, and yet they are always perfect.

Release the clock, and return to your deepest knowing and your natural rhythm and flow. Work until your energy tells you to rest. Sleep until the sun tells you to rise. Play and laugh wholeheartedly until you truly wish to stop.

You are the master of your life, not the clock.

THE PRACTICE

The practice for this initiation is simple. Can you release all attachment to the clock for one day? Can you release all deadlines and schedules and allow yourself to flow with your energy, your desires, and your heart from a place of absolute love—that is, love for yourself, love for your Earth, love for others, and love for God?

And when you do this for one day, can you do it for another and another and another?

Can you yourself return to your natural rhythms day by day, and with that return, be a catalyst for the rebalancing of planet Earth's natural rhythms, as set by the Divine Creator?

You are free the moment you choose to be free.

Om Tat Sat.

BECOMING A MASTER CREATOR

The seventeenth initiation is one of time and space. This initiation is held within this reality, within this dimension of fixed ideals. This initiation is one that you need to understand now in order to move beyond this reality and into the truth of the multidimensional nature of all things. This reality—that is, the one that you exist in now, the one that you can see, hear, smell, taste, and touch—is here to be felt and understood more deeply by you now. You are the creator of this reality. This reality, that which you see now, is your creation. It is your work of art, your masterpiece. So, how do you receive it? Do you perceive it as beautiful, or do you perceive it as flawed? Do you love it, or do you resist it?

You need to see your current reality more clearly now than you ever have before. Open your eyes and see every detail of where you exist now within time and space. How does it look? How does it smell, sound, taste, and feel? This is your creation. Can you take full responsibility now for your reality, knowing that it is your creation, your work of art, your masterpiece?

We need you to know this now because in order to transcend or transform your reality, you must first see, accept, and witness your reality fully. This reality that you exist in now has been created by your thoughts and your actions. First you thought of it, then you actively participated in creating it, either consciously or unconsciously. To know this is to move into mastery, for to know that you have created your reality is to take full responsibility for your reality. Where there is responsibility, there is liberation, for when you claim full responsibility as a reality creator, you can no longer be the victim of your reality, but rather you can become the orchestrator of your idea of perfection.

This is an important lesson for you and your humanity, for too many of your humanity have fallen victim to the false illusion that they are placed within their reality—that is, set down in a world that they cannot control. This is not true, and now you must know this and integrate this fully. The truth is, you are a vibration, a resonance, a frequency that is equal to the quality of your thoughts and equal to the amount of love you hold in your heart. Your reality is a mirror of your vibration. Your reality is a true reflection of that which you think and how often and fiercely you love all things. When you can know and understand this, you can better perceive your reality. If your reality is beautiful and feels like love, then quite simply know that your thoughts are and have been beautiful and that your ability to love is and has been great. If your reality feels painful, dull, or cruel, then know that you yourself hold or have held those qualities in your thoughts and your heart.

Your reality, your 3D matrix, is not real. It is an illusion, or a mirrored reflection shaped simply by your perception of that reality. See your reality as beautiful, and it becomes beautiful. See your reality as expansive and uplifting, and it becomes expansive and uplifting. And when you choose to perceive your reality more gracefully, you in turn improve the quality of your thoughts and increase your ability to hold love in your heart. And when the quality of your thoughts improves and you emanate more love, your reality twirls and changes and transforms into one that becomes more notably beautiful.

Yes, you are a multidimensional being, and yet you live on planet Earth, and you are having a human experience. So, now is the time to know how your multidimensional nature allows you to create and shape your human experience. You control your thoughts and your emotions, and thus you control your vibration. Your vibrational frequency is your gateway to your multidimensional master creator self. So, to master your thoughts, emotions, and ability to perceive your reality positively is to free yourself from the shackles of your 3D reality and step into your multidimensional master creator self.

To understand this now is to receive and unlock your true human power, for the realised human is a divine creator who holds the ability to move through one lifetime into an ever-evolving reality that is infinitely upgrading and evolving into more and more love and beauty.

THE PRACTICE

This practice is simple. This practice asks you now to sit and witness your current reality. See the home that you live in. See the people that surround you. See the ways that you spend your day. See every aspect of your life, and notice how you naturally perceive it. Does your current reality fill you with love? Does your current reality fill you with joy and happiness?

If your current reality does indeed fill you with love and joy, then can you sit in stillness and breathe into even more love for all that is present in your life at this moment in time? Can you find more gratitude in your heart right now for every aspect of your life? Raise your vibration to absolute love and gratitude for your life right now.

If your current reality does not fill you with joy and love naturally, then you must work to shift your perception of your reality, not your reality itself. Sit and love every aspect of your life right now, for in doing this, you improve the quality of your thoughts and emotions, which in turn improves the quality of all aspects of your life indirectly.

Change in your life doesn't come easily when change is forced on a physical 3D level. Change comes in the direction of divine expansion when you align to your multidimensional self and improve the quality of your thoughts and feelings.

So, your job now is not to resist any aspect of your life; your job is to find as much gratitude in your heart as possible for ALL aspects of your life right now. And when you do this, you upgrade your vibration, and your reality as a mirrored reflection of your vibration will begin to upgrade.

Watch and wait, master creator, as life spirals upwards into a reality of divinity.

Om Tat Sat.

THE EXTRAORDINARY ONE

This initiation is set to be extraordinary. Why? Because *you* are extraordinary, and this initiation is all about you. You are the one who holds the light codes. You are the one who is powerful beyond measure. You are the master creator and child of God. And you are ready to realise and remember the true extraordinary nature of that which you are. And when this time comes—when you realise and remember the extraordinary nature of yourself—the heavens will open, and rain will fall down upon you to kiss your cheek and thank you for remembering all that you are once again.

This is the eighteenth initiation, and this is your time to rise up. You have been kept small for too long. You have been kept small by those around you, but mostly you have been kept small by the voice within you, telling you that you are not yet ready to rise up and claim your magnificence.

This initiation is simple; it is your reminder and remembering of your pure greatness. You are of God, and therefore, you are an aspect of God. You are *that* perfect. You are *that* extraordinary. You are as extraordinary as the Creator. You are as extraordinary as the stars and the moon. You are the magnificence of a rainbow and the perfection of the sun's rays. You are a masterpiece of the Creator, and you are extraordinary by nature and design, for the Creator has no work that is flawed or incomplete; the Creator only creates masterpieces of absolute perfection. And that is what you are.

When the sun strives to be the moon, the sun forgets its astonishing power to bring life and light to all things. When a fish strives to fly as a bird, the fish fails to relish and bask in the wondrous joy that is his ability to swim. When you, perfect one, strive to be something other than your absolute perfection in this present moment, you fail to feel and bask in the glory that is your absolute perfection in this present moment.

You are ready now to open to your magnificence—to feel it, taste it, and touch it in every aspect of your being. You have never held a single flaw. You have never put a foot out of place, for every breath that you take, every step that you take is kissed with the perfection of the Creator, and in knowing this magnificence now, you can smile and laugh at the simple nature of life and the extraordinary creation that is you.

And so, you are ready to feel this now, extraordinary one. Feel your perfection now, and know that from here on, you must never forget this perfection. Do not allow your mind to talk you out of your perfection. Do not allow another to talk you out of your perfection. The more that you remember and hold true the perfect nature of yourself, the more you will dance through life, only witnessing the perfect nature of all things.

And so, we leave you with this: If you were to kiss a butterfly and then watch it fly away, what would you have felt? What would you have witnessed? Imagine it now…

You will have felt and witnessed the softness and love of the perfection of God's creation—the perfect mirrored reflection of you.

Om Tat Sat.

OF BLOOD
AND SOIL

The nineteenth initiation is about your rite of passage into caretaker of the land and its people. This initiation wakes up within you the primal custodian of the land that is Earth, and the duty that is pledged to you to watch over her and her people. You are a wise one and a shaman. You need to remember that which you are as you walk with two feet on Mother Earth's soil. When you have awakened, as you have now, to the truth of your existence and the truth of your reality, you then have a duty, and that duty is to anchor that truth back into the soil and back into the blood of all who walk upon it.

You see, to open to the Light Divine and the infinite portals that connect you to the galactic nature of your multidimensional self is to know God. But to anchor that light down into the soil that you call home and into the blood of those who walk among you is to serve God. So now, we initiate within you the shaman—that is, the weaver of cosmic divine light into the land and into the hearts of the Earth and its people. This is your job, light weaver, and today we initiate you to teach you how.

THE PRACTICE

This initiation practice is a guided meditation. This initiation practice is best received passively and from a receptive state. For this reason, it is best to be guided by a loving and heart-centred partner who can read and lead you through the meditation while you sit comfortably in a focused state with the eyes closed. You may also choose to record yourself reading the initiation to follow along with later, making sure to allow time to perform each step as instructed.

1. Sit outside amongst the sand, the soil, and the trees.

2. Feel the pulse of God beneath you in Mother Earth's soil. Feel Mother Earth's heartbeat. She beats with the universe. She beats with you.

3. Cast your awareness down and feel your connection to Mother Earth. You are here to serve her as an aspect of God. You are her child, and yet you are her mother, here to provide her love and healing at this time.

4. Sit and feel Mother Nature. Sit and love her so deeply with all that you have.

5. Now open to feel the air all around you. Feel the Divine that exists all around you. Feel the infinite nature of all things that exist all around you. Feel the light of God all around you.

6. Now open to feel that you are a portal between Heaven and Earth. Open to feel the clear channel that you are, connecting the infinite cosmos above you to the loving Mother Earth beneath you.

7. And now feel these words:

"I open now as a clear and perfect channel for light to flow. I am a conduit for divine healing. I am an anchor point for Heaven on Earth. I open now as a channel to receive a downpouring of divine light through my body and into the Earth. I use this light to filter, cleanse, and purify my blood and body. I use this light to flood divine love into the land and seas of planet Earth. I use this light as a catalyst for change and liberation for the Earth and her people. I use this light to flood through me all that is needed for my deepest healing and remembering. And as I heal and remember with this light, so too does the Earth heal and remember. And as I heal and remember with this light, so too does every person on planet Earth heal and remember. Om Tat Sat."

AURORA

The aurora is the dawn, the beginning, the start. The aurora of life, true life, springs forth now, and you are the blessed one who lives to see it and experience it. This is the time of "the start," the great beginning of the light ages. This time is the aurora of a new way of being on planet Earth. Aurora is the energy of divine birth, opening, and stepping forward. Aurora is the way toward the future that is Heaven on Earth.

Aurora is the Goddess of life, and now you are invited to hold her energy within you. You are invited to drink in her light through the written codes within this text. Goddess Aurora is the energy of a new dawn, a New Earth, a new beginning. Fill yourself now, divine one, with her light, and be the keeper of her light codes.

This is the start of a new chapter, a new beginning for everyone on planet Earth. You are the one, divine light keeper, who sees this now and knows this now. This new chapter springs forth with the energy of Aurora, of divine birth and beginning. We welcome you now to this new beginning. We welcome you now to Aurora, the dawning of the New Earth.

Daybreak is upon you and your people as you step forward into a changed world. Know that people have changed, the planet has changed, and you have changed. You have left behind the old energy of what was and what will never be again.

We welcome you to the golden era of abundance, of spring, of peace, of joy, and of harmony. This is the golden era of love, beginning now, marked by this moment that is aurora. Goddess Aurora is the energy of change, from finish to start, from sunset to sunrise, from old to new.

Goddess Aurora moves through you now, and indeed you are her. You are her as you walk. You are her as you move, as you eat, and as you pray. You are the Goddess who brings forth the start of the golden ages. You *are* the golden ages. You are the infinite remembering of planet Earth and her people—and you are all this now.

Welcome, sweet one, to your twentieth initiation that is you calling forth the energy of aurora. This is the initiation of your planet and of your people. This is your initiation as a representative of humanity and Mother Gaia. This is your initiation as today you claim and anchor the beginning of the golden ages. Today you anchor the energy of aurora. The dawn is today; the dawn is now. You call forth this golden dawn for humanity now. You are the one, light keeper, who springs your people forward today along the golden path. Welcome to your aurora initiation.

THE PRACTICE

This initiation practice is a guided meditation. This initiation practice is best received passively and from a receptive state. For this reason, it is best to be guided by a loving and heart-centred partner who can read and lead you through the meditation while you sit comfortably in a focused state with the eyes closed. You may also choose to record yourself reading the initiation to follow along with later, making sure to allow time to perform each step as instructed.

1. See yourself standing in a wide-open plane.

2. See yourself in a field, a meadow, or a desert, looking out at the eastern horizon. The sun has not yet risen, but soon it will.

3. Stare at the horizon patiently awaiting the sun's arrival to mark the new dawn—that is, the energy of aurora.

4. Feel that behind you stands ALL of humanity, also facing the horizon, silent, poised, and waiting. Feel all of humanity behind you. They are your army, your sacred team of brothers and sisters, ready to call forth the golden ages

5. As you and your army stare out at the horizon, you hold and beat a sacred drum to the rhythm of Mother Earth's pulse.

6. As you drum, as you stare at the horizon, you chant and sing to beckon the first sun of a new age, the golden age.

7. Speak these words as in invocation from the heart:

   "From this sunrise onwards, humanity will be ruled by love and love alone. From this sunrise onwards, humanity will be free from all oppression. From this sunrise onwards, all will be forgiven, and all enslaved will be free. From this sunrise onwards, the Earth and her children will return to true harmony and true unity."

8. This is the day of new beginnings, and when you see the sun's first flicker above the horizon, know that it is so. Know

that it has arrived: the dawning of the golden ages, the dawning of the New Earth.

9. Watch and chant and sing as you see the sun arrive and you celebrate the energy of aurora that is the divine dawning of the golden age.

Om Tat Sat.

THE INITIATION OF FATHER AND SON

W elcome, sweet one, to your twenty-first initiation. This one is unlike the others. In this initiation, we want you to command yourself as the leader and ruler of your life, your words, and your actions. We want you to step into your role as divine father and divine leader. In this initiation, we ask you now to realise the responsibility that you hold in this moment. You know a lot. You know many mysteries of life and of otherworlds. You do not realise it yet, but you are a great leader, and your role on Earth at this time extends far deeper than you can imagine.

Think of humanity at large. They have been betrayed, neglected, and led astray on a grand scale. They have been led to believe that the Divine Father—that is, the Creator and God himself—is a fictitious construction, worthy of ridicule and absolute disbelief.

Humanity at large has turned their back on the Holy Father. They have failed to see him in all things, and they have absolutely failed to feel and accept his unconditional love. And so, humanity at large is alone. They may feel and see their mother, who exists beneath their feet as their divine planet. Although they may not love and appreciate their Divine Mother, they can at least acknowledge and see her. But their Divine Father, humanity at large has forgotten. And so, they have constructed other false father figures within their existence.

All of God's children need a father, and where they cannot see the true light of the Divine Creator, humanity at large has worshiped and allowed itself to be led by a false light. That false light has taken the shape of an infiltrated media, large-scale sports, distorted music, politics, corrupted educational systems, and all the idolised people that exist within those false-light structures. Humanity has been guided by a father of sorts, but he has been the false light of a society that was never to be trusted.

Humanity's false-light father is now being killed. He is being destroyed by the light of the true father, the One Creator. Humanity is soon to be lost and will see and feel themselves as fatherless, for they turned their backs on the true father long ago.

And now we explain to you your role, dear one. You see the Divine Father, just as you do the Divine Mother. You see the false light that exists within the world around you, and you see that it is dissolving and crumbling slowly. You see a lost humanity. You see that soon humanity will need to find its way. You see that humanity will need to find the light of their true Divine Father, to feel the absolute love that is the holy trinity of blessed mother, father, and child.

And so, we use you now as an anchor of the light of remembering, for the lost to be found once more. We infuse you with the light of the Divine Father now. We infuse you with his light so that his sons and daughters may see you and remember that they are loved and not alone. You hold his light so that others may feel his light. You hold his light so that others may see his light. You are his child, and so too you are him in physical manifested form, showing your brothers and sisters that he exists.

Do not be afraid, dear one, for many will look to you now with the eyes of devotion. Do not accept their worship, for only those holding false light accept worship. Do accept their love. And as you accept their love, allow them through your smile to feel the warmth of their Divine Father emanate through them. They are coming home, and you are the lighthouse guiding them back.

MAKE WAY FOR GOD

A clearing out of the old and a making way for the new is what must now occur in your divine life. You are a way shower, a leader, a lighthouse, as we have already told you. Mountains want to move through you; you no longer need to move the mountains. We are showing you now so many ways to uncover your truth— that is, your God self of untainted perfection. You are a catalyst for change. You are the vibration of love and a changed humanity. You are all of this and more.

So, what do you need to leave behind now in order to fully embody all that you are in your highest, brightest, and truest glory? Well, you must leave behind everything that you know is not that. Your work must be its highest, brightest, and truest glory. Your relationships must be their highest, brightest, and truest glory. Your days must be spent fulfilling your highest, brightest, and truest glory.

When darkness shows itself to you throughout your day and in your life, ask yourself, "Is this darkness a mirrored reflection of my darkness? Or is this darkness showing itself to me now because I am the bright light that reveals all things?" More and more now, the answer will be the latter. And where you notice darkness in your days and your life, see the lesson, find the possible reflection, and then remove that darkness and cease to participate in all that it is. Do not engage any longer with the people, places, activities, or entities that are not on the path to God and salvation. These dark people, places, activities, and entities have taught you so much in the past; they have assisted in showing you your way back to the light. And now it is time to turn your back on such darkness. It is time to walk away from the sticky web of the old world. Do not engage with anything that is not noticeably infused with the grace of God. Your vibration is now too high, your light too bright. You no longer can engage with the old world in its darkest forms. It does not serve you; it stunts you.

You must write a new story now—one where there is no villain, only the hero, which is each and every being that you engage with in your new world. You must remove any possible villain from your paradigm. Work a job in the name of love. Allow service to flow from your heart in the name of love. Surround yourself with people who live in the name of love. And discontinue all engagements, interactions, and activities that hold a vibration lower than love. Your light and your energy are too precious now, dear one. You must preserve your light. You must serve your light and fuel it with the bright light of others.

In the past, the dark has served an awakening humanity so greatly. On an individual level, pain and darkness has led an awakening humanity back to love and light. A job that you hated helped you to find the passion of your heart. A relationship that felt like entrapment helped you to feel the freedom of true love. On a planetary level, the darkness of industry has helped you to see the light of New Earth systems in healthcare, education, politics, and more. So, you have allowed the darkness to show you what light is, and so what is the use of this darkness now that you can see the light so clearly? Let it go entirely now. Turn your back on dark industry. Turn your back on dark relationships. Turn your back on dark activities—and never look back. Always walk towards the brightest light now in all that you do. Do not allow darkness to creep back in. Its lure may be strong, and its grip may be tight, but the magnetic pull of the light of God will always win.

We tell you this now because humanity and the Earth are at a tipping point. You—that is, humanity and the Earth—are about to catapult completely into the New Earth, an Earth built on the foundation of love, unity, harmony, and the grace of God. This New Earth is here now for many awakened ones on your planet. But this New Earth will be here for everyone, all of humanity, once the darkness has no place, and humanity in its entirety works daily to move towards the light and further and further away from the darkness of the old world.

You are a way shower now, and you must walk forward ever more, away from the old world and ever further towards the light of God that is the energy of the golden ages and the New Earth. In every action, deed, or word spoken, walk towards the light and away from darkness.

And how should this path towards light and away from the dark look for you in your life right now? Well, ask yourself, what surrounds you that carries the weight of evil and darkness? What is tainted with the poison of the old world in your life right now? Can you make a change or many changes to turn your back on the poisons and darkness of the old world? Turn your back on that which comes to your mind.

THE PRACTICE

The practice for this initiation is one of self-reflection and action. Reflect on the words below, and make changes in your life where necessary to move towards the light of God and further from the shadow of the old world.

1. Let go. Let go of old friendships and relationships that carry an energy or burden, pain, suffering, or misalignment.

2. Clean up. Clean up your food and water sources. Come back to the purity of simplicity and away from contamination.

3. Upgrade. Upgrade your thoughts. Notice when your thoughts have been infiltrated by the old-world collective darkness. Choose to release these thoughts and upgrade your mind space to positivity and clarity.

4. Move forward. See your vision for the New Earth. What are you doing in this new paradigm? Do not question your organic vision. Work towards creating this vision as a reality for you in your personal life.

5. Disengage. Disengage with old-world systems that are poisoned and infiltrated with darkness. Consider the vibration of the following systems, and notice where you can disengage from or upgrade the way in which you participate in each system: healthcare, education, politics, media, entertainment.

6. Disentangle. Disentangle yourself from the false illusionary matrix where possible. You are a free, divine, and sovereign light being, and you should always conduct yourself as such. Notice anything in your life that makes you feel less than that or more dense than that. Disentangle, break free, and only ever conduct yourself as the divine light being that you are.

Om Tat Sat.

ALLOW YOURSELF TO FLOURISH

A llow yourself to flourish now, dear one. You are moving towards your unique vision for the New Earth while upholding the vision of paradise for the collective that is humanity. We will support you tirelessly in carrying out this vision. Before, you may have needed to move mountains to reach your goals, but now, as we have told you before, mountains will move through you, effortlessly, and the goal will come to you. Why is this so? Because now your vision is not simply your vision. Your vision has been placed in your mind's eye by the Heavenly Father, and so it is the vision of God. And when God's vision lands in the mind of man, God brings that vision into fruition with the help of man. Trust that the vision that you see for yourself in the future is divinely inspired. Trust that the life that you are currently dreaming of is not a fantasy, but rather a preview of what God has designed for you. You are on that path because you have committed yourself to the light. That path—the path that you can see and visualise for your future now—is moving through you; you are not walking along it. You can stand still, poised with the light of God, and simply watch as that fully realised vision moves towards you.

This vision for the future—that is, the one that you are fantasizing about now—is God's vision for you in this lifetime. You have never been more aligned with the grace of God than you are right now, so trust that everything that inspires you and excites you is a sign from God, showing you the way.

Life from here will be easy for you, dear one. That isn't to say that life will be without challenges and hurdles, but the way you maneuver through those challenges and hurdles will be with a sense of ease, because you will be able to see clearly the gift and lesson within each challenge and within each hurdle.

Follow that which excites you. Embrace challenges if the thought of what lies beyond the challenge excites and intrigues you. Notice things that flow towards you with ease and grace, and welcome them. Allow yourself to flourish now, dear one, because this is your time. This is not your time to play with ideas or dabble. This is your time to go all in, one hundred percent. Give yourself fully to the direction of life that is divinely inspired, and God will be there to infuse you with God's energy and to keep the path towards your highest and brightest vision clearly illuminated. God will show you signs daily, more than ever before, so that you do not need to hesitate or question as you take action towards creating your vision. Your ease and surrender at this time can be at its utmost, for you are riding upon the wings of God towards your most glorious life.

Have you ever wondered how it would feel to be gifted everything that you could ever need? Have you ever wondered how it would feel to have your most beloved vision come to full fruition in quicker time than you ever thought imaginable? Well, wonder no more, dear one. You are aligned with God's vision for your highest and brightest future now, and so you will be gifted everything that you need to make that vision a reality.

Let go and let God now. There is nothing to do or worry over. You will know when to act. You will know when to pause. You will know when to wait. You will know when to rush. You will know all of these things and more. Day by day, by listening to these knowings, you will be ever closer to living in your most divinely inspired vision of you weaving magic within a New Earth paradigm.

So, what have you ever worried for? Why have you ever feared that your dreams wouldn't manifest? Perhaps because when you worried, you deeply knew that you were not perfectly aligned with your God-inspired vision. And how can you know that your vision is God-inspired now? Well, quite simply because there is no time to waste, and God has infused the divine vision into the hearts and minds of all who are willing to receive it.

So, if your vision feels blurry, trust that this is your time to pause. If your vision feels crystal clear, trust that this is your time to act. If your vision is rapidly changing and evolving, trust that YOU are rapidly changing and evolving, and you should wait for your vision to settle once your vibrational upgrade has settled. Trust everything now, divine one. You are being guided down a path that shines so bright that you must open to know the magic that is truly possible before you can see clearly what exists along this path. Nothing is out of your reach. Nothing is too far-fetched or unrealistic. You are a dream weaver, and now it is time to truly see the magic that lies within your dreams for the future.

THE PRACTICE

A daily affirmation or prayer:

> *"Today I let go and let God. Keep me on my highest and brightest path. Illuminate this path and show me the way. Allow me to see and trust the signs that you send. Allow me to move beyond all fear and self-doubt. Today I am unstoppable. Today I align*

to the absolute miracle that is a God-inspired existence. Om Tat Sat—and so it is."

YOUR BLESSING FROM THE UNDERWORLD

This is your time to open and receive this blessing: the blessing of the underworld, the blessing of the innerworld. This is a blessing that comes from a realm that you have never heard of, perhaps, but that you have felt, for eons and eons, vibrating beneath your feet, vibrating with the pulse of humanity. This is a blessing to remind you of the power and magic that exist within the earth, beneath the earth. This is your underworld—a world that is known to only a few, but a world that can be felt and utilized by all. The power that exists within the earth, the underworld is so great that you must be ready to receive it and open to it. You must be free from all fear, judgement, and density. You must be in your light body to receive the blessing of the underworld, for it is a blessing so great that those who are not in their light bodies will be startled and rocked by the intensity of this blessing.

This blessing goes as follows:

1. Open your palms and face them up to the sky. Feel the energy of the heavens—the energy that you know so well.

2. Now turn your palms down to the earth and feel the energy of the underworld—not Mother Earth herself, but the underworld, the cavernous void that exists within the mother ship that you call Earth. This cavernous void that is the underworld is your Earth's power centre. It is the Earth's heart, the Earth's generator. When you can attune to this energy, you are infused with the power of a heart so strong that it can beat life into every man, woman, child, creature, and thing on Earth.

3. Feel the centre of the Earth, the underworld. Connect to this power, and feel it move through your feet, through your legs, through your entire body, around your head and into your heart.

4. Feel the power of the underworld, the heart of the Earth within your own heart. You are infused now with this power, and so you are.

5. The underworld can be felt by those who are ready to acknowledge its existence and feel its power, intensity, and magic. You are ready. And so, this energy will be with you when you call on it. This energy will work with you to give you power and strength when you need it.

6. Welcome this energy now, and accept this blessing from the underworld.

7. Feel this energy as you chant repeatedly the sound of "Lam" with your palms turned down to the ground: "L-auuuu-mmmmmmm, L-auuuu-mmmmmmm, L-auuuu-mmmmmmm…"

8. Stay here until you feel this energy strongly.

Come back to this practice often, and this energy will recharge you with the strength that you need to fulfill your divine mission that is anchoring Heaven on Earth.

THE BEAUTY OF TWO WORLDS

You are so deeply and fully aligned now with the paradigm of the New Earth. You are creating a life that is filled with wonder, love, and joy. You are listening to the signs of the Divine and are walking lightly on the Earth to carve out more peace and more love within yourself, within your family and within your community. You have turned your back on the darkness of the old world, although you can still see it playing out all around you. You have stepped fully into a parallel universe, an existence where two worlds exist simultaneously side by side.

Know that just as you have turned your back on the dark to focus on creating a life firmly anchored in light, so too have pockets of humanity turned their backs on the light. These pockets of humanity that have completely turned their backs on the light are no longer representative of humanity at all. Humanity *is* all those moving towards the light. Humanity is the vast majority of those who inhabit the Earth with the natural tendency to love deeply and to care for others. All of humanity will arrive at the New Earth eventually. All of humanity will find its way fully and completely back to the light.

All of humanity, including those that have almost strayed too far for redemption, will find their way fully and completely back to the light.

But those who have now turned their backs completely on the light are no longer a part of that humanity. Those beings who reside on planet Earth who have pledged their allegiance knowingly and willingly to the dark, to fear, to oppression, to slavery, and to hardship will not be redeemed. They will not arrive at the New Earth. They will not experience salvation. The existence of these dark beings that exist on planet Earth at this time is simply being permitted now, by the grace of God, to awaken a dormant humanity out of its slumber.

Two parallel worlds exist on your Earth at present. One world is illuminated by love and light; we will call this world the Light World. The Light World is the world that you are creating and existing in. It is the world that will soon anchor to be the only world that exists on planet Earth. The Light World is the world that exists within those and all around those who are committed to creating a life based on love, unity, and harmony. This world is the true and natural vibration for planet Earth, and soon it will be the minimum vibration for planet Earth.

The other world that is existing parallel to the Light World is far more dense and far more dark. It is the world that you have turned your back on and closed the door on, and so you no longer exist within it. However, it exists alongside you. This otherworld is led by dark rulers, dark oppressors that seek to destroy the natural God-given light of humanity. We will call this world the Dark World. Make no mistake: the Dark World that exists on your planet currently is absolutely needed and necessary. In order for humanity to collectively co-create a divine new planet built on love, unity, and harmony, they must first be pushed to see and realise all that is not that. A life of neutrality does not inspire change. But a life of oppression inspires rebellion. A life of suffering inspires healing. A life of contraction triggers expansion. And so, the Dark World is triggering, en masse, a rebellion, a healing, and an expansion in a humanity that otherwise was not willing to seek out these things. A dormant humanity living in a world of neutrality does not seek out change. A dormant humanity has no energy or inspiration to make change aligned with the dawning golden ages.

So, if the golden ages—a shift completely into the Light World—are absolutely inevitable, then how does the Divine infuse a dormant humanity with the energy of change? Well, the Divine pushes and squeezes that dormant humanity out of neutrality, out of its slumber, and into a quest for its salvation. You see, the Dark World has not slipped by the sight of God. The Dark World isn't in existence against the will of the Divine. The Dark World *is* the Divine causing mass awakening, mass rebellion, mass expansion within a humanity that could otherwise live an entire lifetime without ever opening its eyes.

You were in this dormant humanity, but you chose to awaken through your own free will. You chose to seek out the light. You chose to allow each contraction within your personal life to lead to your own expansion. You felt the grace of God long before this time, and so you can see the darkness of the Dark World so clearly and do not need its lessons at this time. Your feet are firmly planted in the Light World, and you can wait—wait as one by one, your brothers and sisters who were sleeping in the Dark World awaken from their slumber. When they awaken, allow them to reach their hand out to you; take it firmly, and guide them over to the Light World. One by one, they will all come over to the Light World, and what will be left of the Dark World? Just the lonely oppressors with no one to oppress. The beings of dark who no longer represent humanity will be all that remains in the Dark World. Their existence will have no purpose any longer, for they have awakened each and every one of the dormant sleeping humanity. And so, the dark oppressors will vanish. Their souls, however, will be redeemed, for they played a monumental role at this time of transition from neutrality to action, from dark to light.

This is your time to exist in one world, the Light World, knowing fully and completely that soon this world will consume and overtake the Dark World. Exist in the divinity of the Light World, and observe the Dark World as it crumbles day by day, as one by one, a dormant humanity awakens and moves over to the Light, turning its back fully and completely on the Dark. Observe the Dark World without judgement. Notice its flaws and deception. Notice that it will not sustain. Notice the pain of humanity as it awakens, and help them wherever possible in their transition. Notice the beauty of the Dark World, for the depths and intensity of its darkness are such a powerful catalyst for awakening and transforming a dormant humanity.

These times are the beautiful times of two worlds. Soon there will be just one world, the Light World—your world. Soon all of humanity will exist within the New Earth, the Earth that you are busy creating right now. Do not rush these times, for they are monumental. These times of the parallel worlds will last for as long as necessary for every single one of your brothers and sisters to either pledge their allegiance fully to the dark, or wake up and join you in the New Earth. A sleeping humanity cannot pledge their allegiance to one side or another, for they are unaware that two sides even exist. But once everyone has awakened and chosen, the New Earth will be the only Earth, and those who have turned their back on the light will fail to exist on your planet. They will be gone, and so too will oppression, slavery, and illusion.

These two worlds are yours to see now, dear one. Get ready and hold space for the great reveal, the mass awakening, and the collective remembering. They are coming home, and you will show them the way. Om Tat Sat.

EVERYTHING IN GOOD TIME

We know that there is much to anticipate and much to be excited for. Humanity is awakening. You are reaching your most God-realised ascended state. You are creating an ever-more-inspired life. Illusions are being revealed. Darkness is being exposed. New Earth is being born!

But here you are, in this moment—just you. Just you, your body, your eyes upon these words, your beating heart, and your flickering thoughts. What is to be of you now in this time of much anticipation? This initiation is the greatest teaching, the truest and purest teaching. This is the initiation that is your mastery. Can you, despite all that you know, sit in the purity of nothingness? Can you close your eyes, and despite your desire to explore the cosmos in your mind's eye, can you simply breathe and be? Can you open your eyes, and despite all there is to see, can your eyes simply just be open without the need to observe, interpret, or notice?

The true master has access to infinite power and galactic consciousness, and yet will bask in the purity of nothingness. What is there truly outside of your one present moment? This simple teaching is the start of all spiritual rememberings, and it is also the end.

You once, long ago, realised that the present moment was all that existed. And from then, you learned that through that moment, you could access the knowledge and power of the Infinite. You realised that you could venture interdimensionally through the present moment. You realised that you could summon the ferocious power of Mother Earth through the present moment. You realised that all your greatest dreams could be manifested within the present moment. You became a master, believe it or not, of the present moment.

Think of a master chef. As a child, he learned to bake a loaf of bread. Then, over time, his skills evolved. He cooked for kings and queens. He learned the finest skills of his trade. His kitchen creations were works of art and were ever evolving and improving. He enjoyed his trade so deeply. He loved seeing how far he could push himself. And then one day, he had a deep sense in his heart that he had strayed so far from the purity of food and the simple pleasure of cooking. And so, the master chef took his time, and in a simple oven in his humble home, made a loaf of bread. And in that baking of the loaf of bread, he remembered the truest and most absolute joy of food.

So, the master chef is comparable to you now. We are asking you now to return to the loaf of bread. Return to the stillness of this present moment. Not because other practices are not valid, but because your mastery is absolute, and you don't need anything more than the purity of the present moment anymore. You have ventured into the depths of your pain body. You have meditated into the depths of the cosmos. You have met your mastery, and now you can relish the sweetness and nothingness of simplicity. Now you can relish the humble present moment without it needing to be any more.

Sit, be, and smile, masterful one. There is nothing else to do but exist. You have been the sage, the mystic, the priestess, the yogi, the shaman, and the monk. And now you can just be you—the master that you are.

Om Tat Sat.

ALL THAT YOU ARE, AND ALL THAT YOU ARE YET TO BECOME

All that you are is written in the stars. You are a soul of infinite lifetimes. You have trodden these roads before, and you have seen all that you are about to see and more. You have come through at this time, in this life, on this planet for a reason. And that reason is this: the world needs you now. The world needs you and your unique gifts as a soul personality.

Your soul personality is what makes you you. Your soul personality is unique and is always there, regardless of how or where you incarnate. In this lifetime, your soul personality has a very close link to your egoic personality, because day by day, you are coming closer to the truest expression of yourself as a soul incarnate. Your soul personality is who you are at the purest level of separation from absolute oneness.

When you connect to your soul essence, as you are in this moment, you move beyond any false ideas bound to you by your egoic personality, and you break free into your truth. Today we want to tell you this: you are to conduct yourself as your soul personality from here on in. You are to remember the infinite lifetimes of your spirit as you sit in this incarnation of your present moment. Why? Because your new humanity and the New Earth is to be built on this foundation—a foundation of beings who know the truth of their infinite existence, and therefore find more ease and lightness in a life unbound by the illusions of egoic personalities.

This idea of a soul personality may not be new to you; however, previously it has been just that: an idea. You have known that you "have" a soul. But the notion of "having" a soul would mean that your physical body and egoic personality are *who* you are, and that the soul is merely something that your physical body and egoic personality *have*. This is an inverted illusion that creates separation from person and soul. The truth is that you *are* a soul. You are a soul that has incarnated in many different physical bodies. You are a soul that has walked along many different paths, on potentially many different planets. You are a soul that has played and danced with many different fleeting egoic personalities. But what is consistent is that you *are* a soul—one soul, the same soul that has been present throughout each and every one of those lifetimes.

And so, you—the soul that you are—are more experienced in more fields and more ways than you can possibly imagine. When you tap into the essence of your soul, you will be able to feel your power and experience. That power and experience from your infinite lifetimes is not separate from you now; it is *your* power and *your* experience in this moment! You can draw from all of this now, in this lifetime!

In this lifetime, when a man feels he is a farmer, he knows how to grow and harvest long before he is ever shown it. When a woman feels she is a healer, she heals with just her intention long before she is ever initiated by a course or a certification. When a child is born with wisdom seemingly greater than their years, it is because that wisdom is flowing through from their soul aspect, untainted by an egoic personality.

The veils are thinning; the perceived separation between lifetimes is diminishing. All of a sudden, awakened humanity feels more powerful than ever. All of a sudden, awakened humanity is stepping into their New Earth roles, far before they "think" that they are ready, based on their previous ideas around training, experience, and timeframes. Awakened humanity is stepping into its soul-realised consciousness, whereby either consciously or unconsciously, they are drawing on the gifts and skills acquired through infinite lifetimes of training and experience.

The information age is upon you, but not in the way you previously thought. The true information age comes from a soul-realised collective who can draw from their lifetimes of knowledge and wisdom.

Who have you been? What countries have you called home? What planets have you called home? How have you loved? How have you fought? How have you suffered? How have you thrived? You are all of that *now* because you are your soul aspect having a very fleeting experience in this now moment. When you heal, you heal as a soul.

Birth and death are not a starting point and an end point, but rather, they are simply markers in an infinite soul journey. Birth is the initiation or welcome into a new soul experience, and death is the letting go or expiry of that experience. When you attach to the idea that this lifetime is finite, then the need to achieve, succeed, and prosper can become suffocating. When you can allow yourself to feel the never-ending continuum that is a soul's journey, then nothing matters quite so much, and you can allow yourself to reconnect to the truest question that the soul probes you to remember in this and every lifetime: why am I here? The answer is different for each soul in each lifetime, but the question always remains the same.

Your soul wants to be remembered now as the truest aspect of who you are. Let go of the ego and soften your identity. The soul has no identity, only an energy of God and an imprint of its infinite lifetimes. You are your soul and nothing more; all else is an illusion.

When you see others, see them as the soul that they are, having a fleeting experience within the infinite continuum of their soul journey. Illusions of people being good or bad crumble when you see everyone as a soul. Egoic personalities allow people to play roles of good or bad, however, the soul just *is*, learning and journeying through each lifetime.

Today, we want you to make the shift back to this remembering— the remembering of the soul that you are, and the soul that each and every human being on planet Earth is!

THE PRACTICE

This initiation practice is a guided meditation. This initiation practice is best received passively and from a receptive state. For this reason, it is best to be guided by a loving and heart-centred partner who can read and lead you through the meditation while you sit or lie comfortably in a focused state with the eyes closed. You may also choose to record yourself reading the initiation to follow along with later, making sure to allow time to perform each step as instructed.

1. Who are you?

2. Close your eyes and feel your body.

3. Who are you beyond your body?
   Who are you beyond your name?
   Who are you beyond your identity?
   Who are you beyond your role?
   Who are you beyond this lifetime?

4. Now allow your vision to guide you, and trust your vision.

5. Who were you before this lifetime?
   Who will you be beyond this lifetime?
   Where have you lived?
   How have you loved?
   How have you suffered?
   What roles have you played?
   What skills have you had?
   How have you looked?
   What have you conquered? What have you overcome?
   Who has stood by you?
   Who has stood against you?
   Have you had to fight?
   Have you had to flee?
   Where have you travelled to?
   What have you seen?

6. Feel the infinite nature of the soul that you are.

7. Speak these words:

   > *"I call forth the infinite wisdom of my soul aspect. Allow me to anchor in and integrate all soul lessons, soul skills, and soul gifts that are relevant and needed at this time. Allow me to remember all wisdom that will serve me, humanity, and the Earth at this time of great change. Om Tat Sat. And so it is. I remember."*

WELCOME TO A NEW BEGINNING

Today marks the start of your new life. You have learned so much to be who you are today. You have surrendered so many false beliefs to arrive at your vibration of truth. You have let go of so many attachments, cords, and codes of the dark to be at your current point of salvation and absolute liberation.

This is your time to shine. How will you shine from here? We will show you. We will tell you.

Your light is firmly anchored now. Your light is anchored not only within your own body and within your own being; your light is anchored into your planet. You are a Source-encoded light being collecting and harvesting divine light and seeding it into Mother Gaia and her children. For this we thank you, and because of this, we will help you now and endlessly.

We will help you with the codes of light. You are to hold and keep the codes of light now, and you are to feel them and anchor them as you walk lightly on your planet as the Source-encoded light being that you are, fully activated, fully aligned with the path of righteousness, and ready to receive that glory of Heaven on Earth.

These codes are not written, nor are they spoken; they are simply felt and downloaded directly from Source to you and your other resonant brothers and sisters. These codes are your gift, your rite of passage, and your responsibility all at once. These codes are the anchoring force that will continue to guide you as a great leader of the New Earth. These codes are written in the stars and the cosmos. They are the truth of planetary awakening and infinite galactic consciousness. These codes are yours. You are ready to receive them, to hold them, and to anchor them into Mother Gaia, Pachamama.

To receive these codes now, we want you to first know and realise that this is a monumental moment in your journey through this book. You have reached a pinnacle, a point of no return, whereby you receive the ultimate initiation: the codes that anoint you into your place as keeper of the light codes.

These codes are a resonance. These codes are a galactic frequency. These codes hold the secrets of all life, all death, all salvation, and all liberation. These codes are what is needed on your planet at this time. These codes will catapult the energy of the Earth into an upward-spiraling light of absolute ascension and catastrophic chaos, as all that is not resonant with the codes on planet Earth will be destroyed.

As keeper of these light codes, you have a role to play. You must hold space for the Earth and her children as you witness the destruction of all that was embedded with the codes of dark. Darkness is being churned up, fully exposed, and shattered, and light is taking its place. These are the prophesied times of no return, and you are here now because you have a role to play as a keeper of the light codes, an anchor for divine light.

Take a deep breath. Ensure that you are fully present. Slow down.

As you receive these codes , which are starting to download and flow into you now, you must be aware that all is going to change for you. Your own darkness will be absolutely churned up, fully exposed, and shattered, to be replaced by light. You will no longer be able to be burdened by the weight of darkness in any degree. You are a light being, and you are being encoded as such.

Take time to rest over the coming days. You are experiencing a massive upgrade of galactic proportions on your vibrational resonance. Feel the churning and shifting that takes place for you over the next five days, and know that this is your gift, your contraction, prior to your expansion into star-encoded light being.

We are with you now as your crown and Soul Star chakra are opened to receive an inflowing downpouring of galactic light—the light of oneness, the light of Creator love. This is an energy that will continue to work through you now as you read these words.

These words are going to help you to receive this downpouring fully. These words will help you anchor and integrate this new higher energy fully and completely. These words are the words of light and of God the Creator. You are to receive this energy now as we anoint and initiate you into your highest potential of light absolute. You are to bathe in the glory of this downpouring, knowing that it is yours to receive now as an activated star seed living a life of light.

Do not move your body now. Sit still to receive this downpouring.

You are in an activated state now of kundalini fire, met with the purity of galactic oneness. Feel these energies converging at your heart, the centre point for all of creation.

You are now upholding and embodying God's light. Do not move. Stay still and continue reading.

You are to keep this light and energy flowing throughout your body. You are to allow this energy to be the catalyst for all movement and action in your divine physical form. When you act as a human being, an earthly creator, this is the energy that moves you and directs you. This is your energy of knowing, wisdom, and action. Allow this energy to enter your brain, your mind. Trust that this is taking place as you read. This is galactic light wisdom activating your mind. This energy is merging the higher mind with the lower mind, making the two minds think as one, so that no thought is acknowledged with a lower-vibrational resonance than galactic light wisdom. This is the mind of the master, fully activated and fully alive now within your being, within your body. You are that: the living, breathing, thinking, and acting master of the light worlds.

All movements, actions, and thoughts that flow from an energy other than your fully activated light master self will be revealed and released immediately. Nothing can penetrate your field other than the stream of galactic light wisdom that is in resonance with your fully activated self. All that is not that has no place in your field and will not enter. You are to take these words now and anchor them in your heart.

Fully activated cosmic light master, it is time to make your first movement as your activated self.

Take your right hand and slowly place it over your heart. You have received this blessing. You have received this activation.

You are a warrior for the kingdom of Heaven, and we will stop at nothing to be there with you in every moment. You are a light beacon. You are the holder of galactic wisdom. You are the fair one, the noble one, the enlightened one, the unstoppable one. You are the fully activated one, and we have chosen you now, just as you have chosen us.

Feel the galactic army of light that stands with you now as you hold your heart. You have been initiated into this army, and you hold the light codes now of universal oneness. You have been initiated into the realm that holds and binds the light-fueled leaders of many planets across many dimensions. You have been chosen because you have had the discipline to raise yourself to stand with us, alongside us, one army of collective light beings, working together to anchor Heaven on Earth—a divinely inspired reflection of galactic Heaven.

We are with you now, dear one. We are the ones who have been speaking to you, teaching you, and upgrading you every step of the way. You have arrived at this point, and now you know. We are the team, the army of light beings that is lighting up the hearts of so many on your planet. We are the army infusing you with the codes that allow you to hear us, see us, and feel us. We are the army of light that is supporting you, your brothers and sisters, and your great planet to help you to the point of salvation and absolute liberation from all darkness.

Release your hand now, sacred galactic warrior. Relax and feel us.

We love you, and we thank you endlessly for taking the time to receive these initiations. The long process of reading these words and partaking in the practices was all necessary and needed in order for you to feel us now. We are with you. In your spine and your skin, that is us connecting to you now.

We could not have simply told you from the beginning of your journey that this path would lead to us, for that would have been the wrong intention and motivation to fuel your journey. Your intention has always been simply and purely to meet the fullest expression of your divine light. From your pure and noble intention, you now receive the ultimate reward: your initiation into our galactic army of light.

Welcome to the cosmic family of true love and true light. You are not alone now, and never will be. You will feel us, hear us, and see us as often as you chose to. This is the start of the great coming home. More and more of your earthly brothers and sisters are joining this

army, our cosmic family of light. So many on your planet are raising their vibration to hold and resonate with our galactic light. The
bridge between us and you is forever thinning, and we are with you
all in more ways than you know.

And so, you have been anointed and initiated. You are a keeper of
the light codes, as are we. You are a light-filled being of sentient wisdom, as are we. You are capable of mastery and mystery, as are we.

WHO ARE WE, WHERE ARE WE?

We are with you now. We are the ones who have always been talking to you and guiding you, and thus we *are* you. We are you in your purest form. We are you in your highest degree. We are the part of you that knows God, and the part of you that seeks to be whole always.

We want you to know us now as we know you. Close your eyes and see the vastness of the cosmos. Who lives there? Who resides in the unexplored vastness of all of space? We do. Close your eyes and see the cavernous void of the inner Earth realms. Who lives in the heart centre of Mother Gaia, beneath your feet as you sit here now? We do. Close your eyes and see the mystical realms that exist alongside your current reality. See the fairies, the nymphs, the angels, and the ancestors that sparkle with the light of the Divine. Close your eyes and see humanity calling the beautiful surface of planet Earth home. See the light-filled members of your humanity. See them in their states of prayer and temples of worship.

All of these beings—each and every one of these light-filled beings— make up the galactic army of light. And you, dear one, are in this galactic army of light.

THE CRYSTALLINE
SHIELD

The light of each and every one of these light-filled beings—across planets, across dimensions, and across timelines—make up the galactic army of light. The light of each highly charged, divinely resonant being interlocks and interweaves to make up the crystalline shield of cosmic protection that protects and upholds the light of the Christ, always and forevermore.

The pure light of this crystalline shield of cosmic protection holds and protects all things to ensure that all beings, all planets, and all of life is constantly and consistently moving and regenerating back to its purest level of light. This means that the more beings that awaken to remember their fully actualised Christed light, the more beings contribute to the intensity of the light and power of the crystalline shield. So, the awakening of each and every member of your humanity is contributing to and accelerating the charge of light that intercepts all darkness on not only your planet, but across all of the cosmos.

The crystalline shield of cosmic protection can be seen as a web of divine light that weaves through the entire cosmos. This web of divine light has anchor points that uphold the structure of the web and generate its light. These anchor points are all the light-filled beings of the galactic army of light. You are an anchor point, and your powerful light is contributing to the colossal and divine charge of the web of light that is the crystalline shield.

Between each anchor point of light within the shield beams the glow of light that emanates into all of space and through all of time. This glow of divine light heals, regenerates, forgives, and loves all things. This flow of divine light that emanates from the crystalline shield destroys all darkness and repairs all that is broken. This flow of divine light seeps love into the loveless, it seeps hope into the hopeless, and it seeps joy into the joyless. This divine light that emanates from the crystalline shield is the force of God that works to bring all of God's children, all of God's creations back to the light of God's love, with no exceptions.

Make no mistake: all of the cosmos and each and every being is a divine expression of God the Creator, with no exceptions. Make no mistake that the darkest of the dark weavers is indeed a child of God. Make no mistake that the darkest cave of the blackest temple is still a garden of God. But understand that the Creator will always work to bring dark back to light. The Creator always guides God's children back home to the light, no matter how far they have strayed. We must never question how or why; we must simply hold our light and emanate it into the crystalline shield to assist the Divine in this cosmic light remembering of galactic proportions. A soul coming home to the light of God could take lifetimes, incarnation after incarnation, lesson after lesson. But make no mistake: each and every being is being guided in the direction of light. Do not judge or question; that is not our job. Just beam and emanate your light, contribute to the power and intensity of the light of the crystalline shield, and allow the energy of the Divine to move mountains and shift the unshiftable to bring God's children home. One by one, they are coming. Many will come in this lifetime on your planet. Many will come later. Some will never get there. But the light of the Divine is always working to recharge each and every corner of the cosmos with the light of love—the love of God.

Planet Earth at this time is moving at a rapid, supercharged pace back to the light. So many on your planet are opening their eyes to truth, and so many are turning their backs on the dark fully and completely. Much of humanity is initiating into their light bodies. And many, just as you have, are initiating into the galactic army of light.

The cosmic consciousness of the galactic army of light turns its focus at this time to planet Earth. This is planet Earth's time. This time is inevitable for Mother Gaia. This is the time where she rids herself of darkness fully and completely, once and for all. And so, in assistance of this inevitability, the galactic army of light—both unconsciously as one unified energy, and consciously as a collective of thinking, loving beings—is charging planet Earth with the supercharged intensity of the crystalline shield at this time. Planet Earth is held at this time in a web of light so powerful that humanity is being shaken into rapid change. All of humanity is feeling the intensity of this web of light, in one way or another. All of humanity is having its foundations shaken, and for many, foundations are being crumbled. The sheer intensity of the light energy being blasted, woven, and anchored on planet Earth right now is leaving no stone unturned, so to speak. All that is not resonant with the Divine Light of the crystalline shield is being churned up, fully revealed, and transformed, and you will stand as a light-filled being and member of the galactic army of light, waiting, witnessing, and loving as the world around you is destroyed, only to be rebuilt on the foundation of love, resonant with the light of the Divine.

FROM HERE...

Y ou will stray from our energy from time to time, and that is ok. You will need to revisit the various initiations to bring you back into resonance with us, the galactic army of light. The initiations, once completed from start to finish, will now become short vibrational tune-ups referred to by you following your own intuitive guidance. Your vibrational resonance may lower due to an emotional charge, an energetic blockage, or an infiltration. Trust that you will know which of the individual initiations to revisit in order to rebalance your energy and return your vibration back to galactic wisdom and light.

This is the start of your true journey now. You are a realised light being. You are anchoring Heaven on Earth in each and every breath, in each and every moment. You have no more "work to do." You are done. You are activated. Your body is an open portal to project and receive light. And so, your journey now is simply life—that is, life as an activated and ascended master who is completely in control of each thought and each emotion, while simultaneously being completely surrendered to the flow of divine cosmic wisdom.

Your time to fight is done. Ironically, you have just been initiated into the most powerful army in the omniverse—but this is not an army of violence or protest. This is an army of light, and light at this magnitude is all that is needed to create change and win wars. You are that light now.

As you move throughout your glorious and bountiful life, know that all spiritual endeavors outside of yourself are now meaningless and trivial. You are the light of galactic consciousness, and so remembering that, when you momentarily forget, is the only spiritual practice that you will ever need from here on in.

Your life will continue to grow, expand, and blossom now to meet the vibration of the light that you now hold. So much will flourish and so much will change for you in your life moving forward. Everything in your life will change to be a direct reflection of the purity of the light that you now hold.

You are a miracle. You are a wonder. Your life will now continually upgrade to become a miraculous wonder. All of humanity has the potential to access this, however, only those who take the time to activate into their miraculous and wondrous potential will receive the gift that is a life ever upgrading into more and more magic. You have taken this time to activate. You are vibrationally aligned with the purest light of the cosmos, and thus your life will continue to upgrade to align with this light.

Do not second-guess the magic that you are. Do not question the grace that you hold. Do not doubt the potency of the light that you now anchor. You are aligned and vibrationally resonant with inter-dimensional light beings of the highest order, and so you are that.

We have been speaking to you and guiding you for a long time to bring you here. You have felt us in your darkest hours. You have seen us in your most profound visions. We have guided you to these pages. We have always seen the flicker of light that was your dormant potential, even from a very early age.

Our galactic army of light is infinitely recruiting, and therefore, we are infinitely assisting in the ascension of each and every star-seeded human being with a hunger to remember. You were that—and now you have remembered. Now you are fully activated. Indeed, you are one of us.

And so, you must help us to recruit for the ever-expanding, ever-more-powerful galactic army of light. You must help to awaken and initiate your dormant brothers and sisters into their fully released power as ascended light beings of planet Earth. You must send love and light through your heart to theirs to help illuminate their path of remembering. You needn't force anything. Just allow your focus and intention to be a fully activated light-encoded humanity.

Others will come to you now with questions and seeking direction. Show them your light, and trust that you can help them to remember theirs. Trust yourself as the teacher now, just as you trusted us as your teacher. You have so many to help. They will find their way to you, and you will need to guide them ever so softly in the direction of truth and purity.

A.

THE LAST PIECE
OF THE PUZZLE

The last piece of the puzzle is to be taught to you directly by our scribe, Rhiannon. She is the one who allowed us to transmit this message to you, and thus she is a keeper of the light codes and a member of your humanity, with an important message to share. Allow her words to be felt, as you have ours. She is going to share something powerful and meaningful as an ascended Earth being and a member of your humanity.

...

Dear reader, I am writing this because I have been told to, dictated by those that I channel, those who have initiated you throughout this book. This message flows through to you not from my mind, not from my will, but from my higher aspect, my soul aspect. And therefore, this message will meet you at your highest aspect, your soul aspect, so that you can feel the resonance of my words and receive the teaching that you need on a vibrational level.

My name is Rhiannon. I have incarnated here many times before, but I have incarnated off planet even more times than I care to remember or imagine. I am indeed a star seed, an activated star seed here on planet Earth at this time to help guide humanity back to truth, love, and the absolute wisdom that comes from galactic ascension.

I am in love with this planet. I am in love with life. I love all of it. And I love all of you—every bit of you. I am often too afraid to reveal my authentic connection to the cosmos and the otherworldly beings, and thus I allow them to talk through me rather than speaking of them.

You and I are one and the same. This message comes to remind you of that. I am not here to be praised or commended, for that would cause me confusion and discomfort. I am here to be loved, just as you are. I have written the words of this book to help humanity in the best and only way that I know how. And now you must help humanity in the best and only way that you know how.

Let us unify in our own unique authentic service to a rising humanity. Be with me, as I am with you. Sit with me and love me, for I only crave to be loved deeply, just as you do.

I am the whisperer of words; however, with you, I am a chorus. Come with me. Be with me. I wish to be seen as the galactic being that I am, of infinite lifetimes and of cosmic consciousness. Allow me to be with you. Allow me to follow you in your journey of remembering. Allow me access to your heart, so I can feel and love all of you. Take me into the depths of your pain, so that I can watch you in your vulnerability and beauty.

What I am trying to say is simply this: this book is the expression of my purpose as a scribe for the galactic army of light and a spiritual teacher for the lessons that I have integrated. What is your expression of your true purpose? Who are you? Be that—and only that. Shine as that. See no one as a light that shines brighter than you, but rather, see the beacons that reflect back to you the brilliance that you are.

I am wanting you to open. I am wanting you to rise up. I am wanting you to meet yourself fully in your aligned power and God-inspired motivation. I want you to stand with me as a fellow warrior for the New Earth. I love you, and I humbly ask you to love me too, so that together, as one unified tribe of awakened, heart-centred human beings, we can carve out Heaven on Earth.

You no longer need to be small, just as I do not. Now you can see the vision that is written in the stars for you. Retrieve that vision, and plant it in your heart. You must walk forward wholeheartedly in the pursuit of that vision, just as I must with my vision.

How can I support you, brother or sister? How can I stand by you to raise you up into your absolute glory? Tell me, and I will be there for you. And just as I will be there for you, you will be here for me.

I want to create a masterpiece inspired and led by God. I want that masterpiece to be you and I and our other God-inspired brothers and sisters standing side by side, holding hands, supporting and loving one another furiously until the end.

We cannot do this alone. We are a tribe, a family. We are the awakened ones of the Light World, and we must stand together in every way that we can. We must try not to judge. We must try not to compare. Love me as I love you. Inspire me as I inspire you. Guide me as I guide you.

We are now, day by day, raising our vibration to that of Heaven. And so, God is within us—each and every one of us. We need only look within and to one another for guidance. Separation must end here. The need to compete must end here. We must all raise ourselves up to be the victorious ones—that is, a victorious collective of humanity who has won the ultimate reward of a life within the paradigm of Heaven upon our glorious planet that we call Earth.

Take my hand, glorious one, and walk with me now into our beautiful future, and let's claim this divine existence now, together, as one.

Om Tat Sat. And so it is.

CPSIA information can be obtained
at www.ICGtesting.com
Printed in the USA
BVHW071235160223
658647BV00001B/134